The Coming Conflict: Antichrist, Affliction, and Armageddon

By Nathan Clay Brummel

Cover design: Holly Root
Print & eBook Design: Glory ePublishing Services

Scripture quotations are from the King James Version Bible (KJV)

ISBN-13: 978-1539734215
ISBN-10:1539734218

CONTENTS

Preface

There is a coming conflict. Already, we can see signs of the times pointing to the second coming of the Lord Jesus Christ. The Bible teaches that the future holds dark days for the church. On the other hand, the Bible also predicts that the saints will do valiantly in the last days.

The children of believers need to be prepared to identify and face the vicious Antichrist, if he should raise his beastly head during their lifetime. The Bible teaches there are certain signs that must appear prior to the return of Jesus Christ. These signs include the great apostasy, the appearance of the man of sin, the Great Tribulation, the preaching of the gospel to the nations, as well as the bowl judgments.

It is dangerous when Bible prophecy is misinterpreted to teach that the future for Christians will be free from persecution and conflict. There are naïve views of the future claiming the world will become Christianized and Christians will be in the ascendancy in politics and every other sphere.

We, as believers, need to fight against the spirit of Antichrist, which is already at work. Already, there are many "antichrists" with a lower case "a."

The future that will soon unfold is the story of the triumph of the Lamb over the Dragon, Antichrist, False Prophet, and the Great Whore. Faithful believers will face a short time of severe tribulation, but after the affliction, they will be invited to the marriage supper of the Lamb.

The afflictions the church will endure in the future are nothing compared to the weight of glory she will experience as she drinks of the River of Life in the Paradise of God. As a Christian, it is critical in these last days that you meditate upon and cling to your future hope so you will be willing to suffer and sacrifice for the cause of Christ in this last bitter conflict.

32. Remember Lot's wife.

33. Whosoever shall seek to save his life shall lose it; and whosoever shall lose his life shall preserve it.

34. I tell you, in that night there shall be two men in one bed; the one shall be taken, and the other shall be left.

35. Two women shall be grinding together; the one shall be taken, and the other left.

36. Two men shall be in the field; the one shall be taken, and the other left.

37. And they answered and said unto him, Where, Lord? And he said unto them, Wheresoever the body is, thither will the eagles be gathered together.

CHAPTER 1

Left Behind!

The first book in the best-selling series by Tim LaHaye and Jerry Jenkins has the dramatic title, *Left Behind*. The *Left Behind* series has sold more than 10 million books. The tale begins with a gripping story of Christians being raptured out of a jet on a transatlantic flight. In the middle of the night, one hundred people on the jet disappear, leaving their clothes, rings, and watches behind on their seats!

The rest of the passengers (along with the pilot) are left behind! It soon becomes evident that all around the world, the Christians have disappeared. Young teenagers, as well as children, who the authors refer to as "the innocents," also disappear.

Immediately following this rapture, an unknown Romanian named Nicolas Carpathia becomes the president of his country. Powerful financial interests supporting world economic unity give Carpathia their backing and even the United Nations stands behind this man who is soon revealed as the Antichrist.

The Secret Rapture of Dispensational Premillennialism

The theology behind the *Left Behind* series is dispensational pre-millennialism. Initially, the teaching of a rapture seems Biblical. In Luke 17, Jesus taught that two men would be in bed; one will be taken, and the other left behind. He spoke of two women who would be grinding; the one would be taken, and the other left behind. So the Bible does teach a sort of "rapture" in the sense that Christ will suddenly re-appear and take His elect to be with Him in the sky, while initially leaving behind the reprobate.

The most striking feature of dispensational pre-millennialism is that it places the rapture of the saints prior to the Great Tribulation. The hope of those who believe in the rapture is that they will be taken out of the world so they avoid the Great Tribulation under the Antichrist.

However, this is an illusory hope. The Bible teaches that Christians will suffer during the tribulation. This is precisely why Jesus tells us about a great tribulation that will be "such as was not since the beginning of the world to this time, no, nor ever shall be" (Matthew 24:21).

The rapture is an important event in the system of eschatology believed by dispensational pre-millennialists. They have popularized the idea of a secret rapture. Pre-millennialists believe Jesus will return prior to a thousand-year rule on planet Earth. The basic problem of historic pre-millennialism is that it wrongly interprets the "thousand years" in Rev. 20:1-7 in a literal way. Later on in this book, we will deal with the idea of the millennium and examine the symbolism of the number 1,000 in this context.

Dispensationalism is a radical form of pre-millennialism.

Historic pre-millennialism does not advocate a rapture. Dispensationalists divide history into seven distinct periods. They claim God deals with men differently in these dispensations. The seven dispensations are innocence, conscience, human government, promise, law, grace, and kingdom. They teach a basic difference between the kingdom people (the Jews) and the church (the Gentiles).

By the rapture, they mean "the sudden, secret coming of Christ to take unto Himself in the air the living saints and the saints who are resurrected at this time." The rapture is a secret, silent coming of Christ.

In the book *Left Behind,* the disappearance of the saints is something so quiet and unannounced that some people do not realize what has happened. One man has drunk too much and is fast asleep on the plane. Another man supposedly feels his wife get out of bed, but later finds that she has disappeared.

The word "rapture" literally means "to seize" or "to carry away." That is why the word evolved to mean "rapture" in the sense of being carried away with pleasure or delight. Since Christ will seize or carry away the saints, the event has been called "the rapture."

According to those who believe in this secret rapture, this sudden, unannounced disappearance of the saints from the earth could happen at any time. Tomorrow you could be driving home from work and be raptured and your car would continue on without you. Perhaps you have seen the bumper sticker: "If you see this car going down the freeway without a driver, I've been raptured."
Dispensationalists can be very dramatic:

> One of these days, as sure as this is the Word of God, those who have pled with you, who have warned you, who have prayed for you, will be missing. The preacher

will be gone, mother will be gone, wife will be gone, and babies' crib will be found empty. Imagine getting up some morning and your wife is not there, and you call for her, but there is no answer. Hundreds and thousands are calling the police, jamming the telephone lines.

Those who believe in this rapture believe in three comings of Christ. The first coming is the rapture. This is called "the coming of Christ for His saints." The saints will suddenly depart out of the world for seven literal years. The second coming is "the revelation" after seven years. The third is the final coming.

The most troubling aspect about the pre-millennial dispensational understanding of the rapture is it teaches that saints will be taken out of the world prior to the coming of the Antichrist and the Great Tribulation. Therefore, the church will escape the terrible sufferings and persecutions at the end. The church will never have to face the Antichrist.

This is *the illusory hope* of the rapture. Many hope they will be taken away before the last final evil days come. Do not be deceived; it is an illusion. There will be one last battle for Christians to fight by faith.

No Secret Rapture, But a Noisy Public One

The Rapturists pin their hopes on I Thessalonians 4:15-17 where the Apostle Paul writes about the second coming of Jesus:

> For this we say unto you by the word of the Lord, that we which are alive and remain unto the coming of the Lord shall not prevent them which are asleep. For the Lord himself shall descend from heaven with a

shout, with the voice of the archangel, and with the trump of God: and the dead in Christ shall rise first: Then we which are alive and remain shall be caught up together with them in the clouds, to meet the Lord in the air: and so shall we ever be with the Lord (I Thessalonians 4:15-17).

But the Bible teaches that Christians are not going to be raptured out of the world prior to the great tribulation. In fact, in I Thessalonians, we find that there is no such thing as a secret rapture. Here, the Apostle Paul is correcting an error of some in Thessalonica. Some thought that those who had already died would not be resurrected to eternal life. But Paul responds that those who are alive at Christ's return will not have an advantage over those who have died in Christ.

When Christ comes, we are not going to precede the dead saints in any way. The dead in Christ will rise first and then those who are alive will be caught up with them unto Christ in the sky.

We have come to what has been called the noisiest verse in the Bible. I Thessalonians 4:16 is called the noisiest verse in contrast to the supposed secret, quiet, unannounced rapture! Notice the noise: "For the Lord himself shall descend from heaven with a shout, with the voice of the archangel, and with the trump of God: and the dead in Christ shall rise first" (I Thessalonians 4:16). Thus, the Bible teaches that the disappearance of the saints will be a very public event; Christ will descend from heaven with a shout. The trump of God will resound. This is no silent appearing – it is a public, noisy second coming.

A Timely Argument and Warning

False teachers had overly excited the Thessalonians and shaken them into thinking that Christ could come at any moment. Some of the Thessalonians had even stopped working or sold their possessions. Why should they not anticipate a sudden departure out of the world?

The Apostle Paul warns: "Let no man deceive you by any means: for that day shall not come, except there come a falling away first, and that man of sin be revealed, the son of perdition" (II Thessalonians 2:3). Paul believes in one final coming by Jesus after the saints have suffered under the apostasy and persecution of the Antichrist. He gives these two reasons why Christians should not believe in a rapture that could occur at any moment.

Looking at the first reason, "except there come a falling away first," Paul says Christians should not think the day of the Lord has come because the great apostasy has not occurred. Paul's second reason is "and that man of sin be revealed, the son of perdition." Indeed, the son of perdition, the Antichrist has not yet come!

All pre-tribulationists believe the Antichrist will be revealed after the rapture. In other words, they say the church will not be here when the Antichrist comes. The Christians will be taken out and then the beast will raise his ugly head.

However, if believers would not be around to see the Antichrist, why then would Paul try to convince his readers the day of Christ has not come by pointing out that Antichrist was not yet there? If he believed in a pre-tribulational rapture, all he would have to say is that the day of Christ has not yet come because we Christians are still here on planet Earth!

Paul carefully describes the man of lawlessness. The natural assumption is that the apostle describes the Antichrist carefully because he wants Christians to be able to identify the man of sin when he appears. The point is not that Christians will go to heaven prior to the appearance of the Antichrist, but that Christians should recognize the one whose number is 666 when he appears. The church should not be deceived into thinking she will be raptured out of the world prior to the terrible things that will happen during the tribulation.

Jesus taught about His second coming and how the saints would be taken up in Luke 17:34-36:

> I tell you, in that night there shall be two men in one bed; the one shall be taken, and the other shall be left. Two women shall be grinding together; the one shall be taken, and the other left. Two men shall be in the field; the one shall be taken, and the other left (Luke 17:34-36).

Just because we do not believe in a pre-tribulation secret rapture does not mean we do not believe Christ will not seize believers at the end and leave the wicked behind. He will. Jesus clearly teaches that He will return and take the saints initially, leaving the wicked behind.

Christians may be flying over the Pacific Ocean on a jetliner and suddenly, the bright light of Christ returning will shine. All will see this last sign of the return of Jesus, the sign of the Son of Man Himself. It is true that the Christians on the plane will be taken first. Similarly, vehicles will be driving around Chicago, as they do night and day. When Christ returns with a shout, He will take the Christians out of their cars, which will crash into cars still being driven by the wicked.

Until the end, the children of God and the children of the Devil will be living and working together. Humanity is one organism. Paul would say: You cannot go out of this world. Even though many Christians will have to flee to the mountains during the Great Tribulation, the believers will still be intermixed somewhat with unbelievers. But when Jesus comes, that seeming unity will be disrupted.

Jesus will send His angels to take His saints out of the wicked world and fold them in His bosom. The original Greek uses a very nice word for the word "taken." It means to take to one's self, to enfold in one's bosom. The Great Shepherd will fold His sheep and lambs into His bosom. He will take them to Himself in the sky. Christians will be taken from their cells, torture chambers, and from their hiding places in the mountains and caves.

On the other hand, the word "left" is terrible. It sounds weak in our English translation. Literally, the word means "to send away" or "to dismiss." Elsewhere, it is translated as "reject" or "cast away." It could be that the nuance is that Christ will leave the reprobate wicked whom He actually casts away from Himself.

Jesus will make an absolute separation. He will forever split asunder the human race; the elect will be caught up to Heaven, and the reprobate thrown into Hell. The one shall be taken and the other left, rejected, and cast away.

Life will be going on as usual in the world when Christ returns. On the half of the globe where it is night, two men will be sleeping and one will be taken while the other is left behind. Both men will wake to the sound of a trumpet, but the one will be whisked away by the angels.

On the other side of the globe where it is day, people will be going about their work, whether two women are grinding together or men are working in a field. Christ presents life in its normalcy. Especially to the wicked,

Christ's arrival will be like that of a thief in the night. His arrival will surprise. Life will seem to be going on as usual, and then the final separation will occur.

Christians who live immediately preceding the return of Christ will experience dark, awful days. Paul teaches that there will be days of apostasy and evil.

I would dishonor God's Word and do you a disservice if I did not equip you to recognize the Antichrist if he appeared during your lifetime. He will be an individual person. He will be a man. His doom is sure, for he is the "son of perdition." He will become some kind of world-church leader. In the last days, there will be a great apostasy: "And because iniquity shall abound, the love of many shall wax cold" (Matthew 24:12).

At the end of the Great Tribulation, Christ will come again with His mighty angels to judge the nations and redeem His church. Christ's appearance will surprise the wicked.

The people of Sodom lived in such worldly-mindedness that they all perished when God destroyed the city with fire and brimstone. Before the flood, the great masses were completely engrossed in earthly affairs. It was business as usual. Since they were attached to worldly things, judgment overtook them suddenly and unexpectedly without hope for deliverance.

Just as these judgments of God surprised impenitent mankind in the past, so Christ's judgment will take place without any preceding indication of its day or hour. Christ does teach that there will be perceptible signs of His return. But the signs of apostasy and Antichrist will indicate only in a general way the approaching end. It will be impossible to prophesy the actual year, day, or hour of the return of Christ. His return will take place suddenly and unexpectedly and those who have not prepared for it will be irretrievably lost.

In a few powerful words, Jesus gives us something to remember. He warns: "Remember Lot's wife." Jesus wants us to remember a historical incident connected with God's destruction of Sodom. God told Lot and his wife not to look back at Sodom. But Mrs. Lot was sinfully attached to worldly things. Her attachment to the wickedness had fatal consequences. She looked back with longing eyes and was immediately killed. She turned into a pillar of salt.

The history of Lot's wife should warn us not to remain attached in our hearts to the pleasures of this sinful world. The urgent question for you is: Are you prepared for Christ's coming? Will you be left behind?

Our Savior uses just three words to warn us: "Remember Lot's wife." What a warning these words contain. Watch, therefore. Do not be a worldly Christian. Remember Lot's wife. Believe that the crucified Jesus will return to judge the living and the dead.

6. And ye shall hear of wars and rumours of wars: see that ye be not troubled: for all these things must come to pass, but the end is not yet.

7. For nation shall rise against nation, and kingdom against kingdom: and there shall be famines, and pestilences, and earthquakes, in divers places.

8. All these are the beginning of sorrows.

9. Then shall they deliver you up to be afflicted, and shall kill you: and ye shall be hated of all nations for my name's sake.

10. And then shall many be offended, and shall betray one another, and shall hate one another.

11. And many false prophets shall rise, and shall deceive many.

12. And because iniquity shall abound, the love of many shall wax cold.

13. But he that shall endure unto the end, the same shall be saved.

14. And this gospel of the kingdom shall be preached in all the world for a witness unto all nations; and then shall the end come.

15. When ye therefore shall see the abomination of desolation, spoken of by Daniel the prophet, stand in the holy place, (whoso readeth, let him understand:)

16. Then let them which be in Judaea flee into the mountains:

17. Let him which is on the housetop not come down to take any thing out of his house:

18. Neither let him which is in the field return back to take his clothes.

19. And woe unto them that are with child, and to them that give suck in those days!

20. But pray ye that your flight be not in the winter, neither on the Sabbath day:

21. For then shall be great tribulation, such as was not since the beginning of the world to this time, no, nor ever shall be.

22. And except those days should be shortened, there should no flesh be saved: but for the elect's sake those days shall be shortened.

CHAPTER 2

The Signs of Jesus' Return

J esus' disciples were caught up with Jewish dreams. Assuming that the two events would happen simultaneously, the disciples asked Jesus what the sign of the destruction of the temple and the end of the age would be. Jesus had said that not one stone of the temple would be left upon another. The disciples had Jewish dreams of a powerful, carnal kingdom on earth, ruled by Jesus. But Jesus' response was, "My kingdom is not of this world" (John 18:36).

The Jewish dreams of the disciples for an earthly, millennial kingdom find expression today in both pre-millennialism and post-millennialism.

Today, the post-millennial dream of a kingdom of Jesus on earth is nothing more than a contemporary expression of Jewish dreams. Post-millennialists believe the earth will become Christianized. The future for Christianity and the church is one of spectacular growth and worldwide influence. In order to justify this belief, the post-millennialists twist Jesus' prophecies in Matthew 24 to achieve their vision of a future, carnal kingdom.

The Error of Preterism

Post-millennialism is the view that Jesus will return only after His rule has been universally established. Post-millennialists believe Christ's Kingdom will eventually triumph in the world. "Post" means "after:" Christ will come after a glorious millennial kingdom has been established on earth.

Preterism, a form of post-millennialism, is the view that all or nearly all the events foretold in Matthew 24 have already come to pass and all we have to look forward to is the return and the final judgment. Examples of preterists are R.C. Sproul (of Ligonier Ministries) and Gary DeMar (a Christian Reconstructionist).

The word "preter" means past or before. The dictionary defines a preterist *as a person whose chief interest and pleasure is in the past.* "Preterism" refers to "what has already taken place."

In theology, a preterist is one who believes the prophecies of the books of Matthew and Revelation have already been fulfilled. Preterists believe the events predicted by Jesus in Matthew 24 occurred in connection with the fall of Jerusalem to the Romans in A.D. 70. They teach that the saints can expect an earthly victory in the future. The majority of the human race will be converted, and the world will be "Christianized." Christians will control all aspects of cultural and national life.

Preterists also believe that there will be no great apostasy from the Christian faith in the future. Instead, they argue that the abomination of desolation that Jesus predicts refers only to the desecration of the temple by the "idolatrous ensigns" of the invading Roman army in A.D. 70. Along with this, they argue that the great tribulation mentioned in Matthew 24:21 refers to the suffering of the Jews at that time.

Furthermore, preterists believe the Antichrist will not appear before the millennium and the false prophets and false christs of Matthew 24:24 refer only to the pretender-messiahs and false teachers among the Jews.

For the preterist, the preliminary signs mentioned in Matthew 24:29 are not the literal darkening of the sun and moon prior to Jesus' second coming, but the going out of the figurative light of the Jews as a nation in A.D. 70. For instance, Marcellus Kik interprets Jesus' words, "Immediately after the tribulation of those days shall the sun be darkened, and the moon shall not give her light" to mean that "The sun of Judaism has been darkened."

They continue to argue that the events of verse 29, namely, the shaking of the powers of the heavens described by Jesus, "refers to Satan and his angels."[1] They say that the coming of the Son of Man described in verses 27 and 30 is not the visible, bodily return of Christ, but His revelation in the apostolic preaching of the gospel. The gathering of the elect by the angels in verse 31 is the spiritual saving of the elect through the gospel. The "angels" are human preachers.

The preterists find the basis for their interpretation in Matthew 24:34: "Verily, I say unto you, This generation shall not pass, till all these things be fulfilled." They claim that "this generation" must refer to the generation Jesus is addressing. This means every single prophecy of Christ in Matthew 24:4-31 was fulfilled exhaustively in the lifetime of the generation alive at the time of Jesus' instruction. Nothing foretold in verses 4-31 pertains to the second coming.

Post-millennial Reconstructionist Gary DeMar agrees: "These chapters have nothing to do with when Jesus will return at the final judgment. There are no observable signs leading up to His bodily return."

---

[1] Marcellus Kik, *An Eschatology of Victory*, 133.

This is also the position of J. Marcellus Kik in his book, *An Eschatology of Victory*. The "end of the age" (Matthew 24:3) means the end of the Jewish age, which is followed by the age of the church.

The Exegetical Poverty of Preterism and Post-millennialism

It is no wonder that the Reformed believer views preterism as an astonishing position! Especially, when one considers that Antichrist, the great apostasy, the abomination of desolation, the great tribulation, the coming of Christ in the clouds, and the angels gathering in the elect, are all a part of the past. Where does that leave us?

Chapter 11 of the *Second Helvetic Confession* (1566) demonstrates that preterism is not the historical Reformed position in the following excerpt:

> And from heaven the same Christ will return in judgment, when wickedness will then be at its greatest in the world and when the Antichrist, having corrupted true religion, will fill up all things with superstition and impiety and will cruelly lay waste the Church with bloodshed and flames.

How should we understand Jesus' teaching in Matthew 24? How should we understand the "generation" mentioned in Matthew 24:34: "Verily, I say unto you, This *generation* shall not pass, till all these things be fulfilled."

The natural sense of "this generation" is the normal lifespan of those to whom Jesus preached. The King James translation "be fulfilled" could be misleading because it implies that these things would occur fully or exhaustively during the span of that generation.

The Greek is simply "...*till all these things happen.*" "All these things" are the things that have to do with the destruction of Jerusalem *and* the second coming of Christ. All these things would happen, but *they would happen typically, or in the historical type!*

The destruction of Jerusalem was a God-ordained historical type of the final judgment. It was merely typical! Not exhaustive! Not the reality! The reality was still in the future. As is always the case with types, the destruction of Jerusalem came far short of complete fulfillment of the deliverance of the saints in the way of judgment.

God had promised to Abraham that His seed would inherit the land of Canaan. When the Israelites entered Canaan, this prophecy was fulfilled. But it was not fulfilled exhaustively. It was not fulfilled in reality. This only occurs when the seed of Abraham inherits the heavenly Canaan.

Scripture often presents prophecy with type and reality interwoven throughout. By the process of prophetic foreshortening, the widely separated mountain peaks of history merge and are seen as one. Here, two momentous events are intertwined, namely, the judgment upon Jerusalem (its fall in the year 70 A.D.) and the final judgment at the close of the world's history. God's judgment of Jerusalem is a type of His judgment of the whole world.

Therefore, in Matthew 24, Jesus is painting the final judgment in the same colors as the coming destruction of Jerusalem. The pagan altar and the swine offered upon it in the 2nd Century B.C. by Antiochus Epiphanies pointed ahead to Antichrist and the abomination of desolation he will set up. Likewise, the idolatrous legions of Rome committing sacrilege in the temple foreshadows the great and final violation of all that is sacred by the Antichrist.

In Matthew 24:14, Jesus speaks of the gospel being preached to the nations: "And this gospel of the kingdom shall be preached in all the world for a witness unto all nations; and then shall the end come." It is hard to imagine how we can conceive of this as fulfilled by 70 A.D. The preterist must interpret this prophecy of the gospel going to the nations as fulfilled already in the lifetime of the Christians who lived to see the destruction of Jerusalem.

It is hard to see how the prediction that angels would gather the elect from the far corners of the earth could have been fulfilled at the time of the destruction of Jerusalem. The claim that the angels gathering souls from the far corners of the earth simply is symbolic of Christian preachers preaching is eisegesis.

It is difficult to see A.D. 70 as involving the coming of Jesus on the clouds of Heaven as is described in verse 27: "For as the lightning cometh out of the east, and shineth even unto the west; so shall also the coming of the Son of man be." Jesus predicts His glorious bodily return which certainly did not happen in A.D. 70 (although it is true that Christ came in judgment upon an Israelite nation who had rejected the King of the Jews).

Preterists are forced to make two different comings of Christ out of the identical mention of His coming in Matthew 24:27 and 24:37. Their ironclad rule is that everything before verse 34 of Matthew 24 refers only to the destruction of Jerusalem. But in verse 37, the reference is to the second, bodily return of Jesus. However, a rule of exegesis is that the same word, in the same context, must mean the same thing, unless something clearly makes this impossible. Listen to the lofty language that Jesus uses to describe His return:

> For as the lightning cometh out of the east, and shineth even unto the west; so shall also the coming of the

Son of man be. For wheresoever the carcass is, there will the eagles be gathered together...And then shall appear the sign of the Son of man in heaven: and then shall all the tribes of the earth mourn, and they shall see the Son of man coming in the clouds of heaven with power and great glory (Matthew 24:27- 28, 30).

This language simply cannot by any process of imagination or interpretation refer to a mere judgment of Jerusalem. If this lofty language refers to nothing more than Jerusalem's destruction, then, by the same process of reasoning, the very similar words of Matthew 25:31-46 must also be given this restricted interpretation. In both cases, the Son of man appears in great glory and His people are gathered before Him. Both clearly refer to the personal return of Jesus Christ.

The most significant problem for preterists is that, under the preterist interpretation, the disciples' question about the end of the age is not really answered and the chapters most Christians have always looked to for teaching about the Lord's return are not about the Lord's future return at all. In fact, Jesus has virtually nothing to say about His second coming if we restrict the interpretation as preterism does.

The preterist interpretation of Matthew 24 is a daring attempt to save the post-millennial vision of a future, earthly, carnal kingdom. It would be a stunning coup, if preterists could prove that apostasy and persecution were all part of the past.

But this coup cannot be carried off. In Matthew 24, our Lord Jesus Christ teaches exactly the opposite. He says that His church can expect struggle and persecution as the world becomes increasingly evil and hostile. The post-millennial interpretation is a failure. Worse yet, it leads to a false doctrine that makes the Lord predict the very opposite for His true church than what He actually did forecast. Christ promises a spiritual victory through tribulation, not an easy earthly victory within an earthly Christian kingdom.

Christ and His apostles warn the church that she must expect hard struggles in the last days. She will need to do battle with heretics and false christs. The church needs this warning.

Signs That Are Not Imminent

Jesus teaches His disciples there are signs that are not imminent signs. An imminent sign is one revealing that the return of Jesus is close at hand, impending. There are other signs that point to the return of Jesus, but do not reveal it as happening within a few years. One cannot interpret certain signs as infallible indications that the end of the age is immediately in sight. This is the idea of Jesus' phrase: "the end is not yet" (Matthew 24:6).

Jesus predicts various coming events like the arrival of false christs, wars and rumors of wars, famines, and apostasy. He declares that all of these signs will be only the beginning of woes or birth pangs. The "end" about which the disciples have asked "is not yet."

Birth pangs are only the first sign that a baby is going to be born. At first, the birth pangs are not so great; they are farther apart in time. The birth Jesus has in mind is the rebirth of Heaven and earth.

The destruction of Jerusalem is a particularly terrible example of the birth pains Jesus predicts. This judgment executed upon the Jewish nation was a type, a foreshadowing, of the final judgment. About 70 years after the birth of the Lord Jesus, the Roman general Vespasian marched on Jerusalem. His son Titus took charge of the attack after Vespasian returned to Rome to be crowned emperor. Jerusalem was crowded with pilgrims during the

Passover. The Jewish people had cried out before Pilate, "His blood be upon us and upon our children!"

Christians remembered Jesus' teaching in Matthew 24 and fled the city of Jerusalem, taking refuge in the city of Pella. Back in Jerusalem, conditions were frightful with religious disputes between the Zealots and the Jewish leaders. The result was rebellion against Rome. Titus conquered the city. The Roman legions massacred the Jews. Daniel 11:31 was fulfilled when the continual burnt offering was taken away. The temple was burned after a Roman soldier tossed a burning torch through one of its windows.

The apostles wrote of the presence of false prophets in the last days. Peter says: "But there were false prophets also among the people, even as there shall be false teachers among you, who privily shall bring in damnable heresies" (II Peter 2:1).

Paul states, "Now the Spirit speaketh expressly, that in the latter times some shall depart from the faith, giving heed to seducing spirits, and doctrines of Devils" (I Timothy 4:1).

The Bible does not teach that there will be an increasingly successful spread of the truth toward the end. Rather, there will be increasingly entrenched unbelief.

These signs will grow in intensity as the end approaches. Their growing intensity will be a sign of the approach of Christ as by these events, the end of the age is foreshadowed and brought closer. God's eternal plan is being carried forward.

As the time of childbirth approaches, the mother experiences more and more intense and frequent birth pangs. Likewise, toward the end of the present age, these signs will be more numerous, extensive, and fearful than ever before. The final outbreak of these terrors will be a sign of Jesus' imminent return.

Imminent Signs

Jesus predicts the worldwide spread of the gospel as an imminent sign. He becomes more definite about when the end will come. It will be after the gospel has been preached to the nations: "and then shall the end come" (Matthew 24:14). The worldwide preaching of the gospel may be considered the first of the definite preliminary signs.

The Great Tribulation is another one of the signs of Jesus' imminent return. What Jesus says about great signs in the heavens immediately following the Great Tribulation demonstrates He is talking about a Great Tribulation that happens right before the end: "Immediately after the tribulation of those days shall the sun be darkened, and the moon shall not give her light, and the stars shall fall from heaven and the powers of the heavens shall be shaken" (Matthew 24:29).

An important imminent sign is the arrival of the final Antichrist (Matthew 24:23-24). During the Great Tribulation, the Antichrist will set up the Abomination of Desolation (Matthew 24:15). The Antichrist will set himself up in the temple of God. Jesus states this final bitter attack upon God's elect will be of a very brief duration. In Revelation, the reign of the Antichrist is symbolized by a seven-year time span.

The final imminent sign of Jesus' return is the sign of the Son of Man in the sky. Jesus speaks of the appearance "of the sign of the Son of Man in heaven: and then shall the tribes of the earth mourn, and they shall see the Son of man coming in the clouds of heaven with power and great glory" (Matthew 24:30). This sign will be the immediate precursor of Jesus' return: with this sign, Jesus Himself will return publicly and visibly for the world to see.

The Lessons for Us

It is the cross that defines history for the Christian. Jesus had to teach His disciples that what would characterize their King and the citizens of the kingdom in this world would be suffering.

The Bible teaches a theology of the cross, not a theology of glory. The writer to the Hebrews exhorts the disciple of Jesus: "Let us go forth therefore unto him without the camp, bearing his reproach. For here have we no continuing city, but we seek one to come" (Hebrews 13:13-14).

The future for Christians in this world contains the certain prospect of cross-bearing. We do not look for glory here. Christians in the last days will need to take up their crosses and follow Jesus. They will need to sacrifice their lives. The world is not getting better. The Antichrist's henchmen will torture Christians as they have never been brutalized before. The development of new technologies does not mean that the world is getting morally better. Rather, new technology will be used to torment those who confess that Jesus alone is Lord.

The Bible teaches that Christians suffer for the kingdom in this fallen world. Paul prays that believers "may be counted worthy of the kingdom of God, for which ye also suffer" (II Thessalonians 1:5). In the last days, he predicts that the saints will be *troubled*: "And to you who are *troubled* rest with us, when the Lord Jesus shall be revealed from heaven with his mighty angels" (II Thessalonians 1:7).

It is the cross, not glory that defines the kingdom of Jesus in this fallen world. Therefore, expect suffering and persecution as Jesus predicted. Watch out that no one deceives you. Jesus has a great deal to say about deception in this discourse. He says that if anyone says to you, "Look, here is the Christ" that you are not to believe it. He talks about how false prophets will perform great signs and miracles to deceive even the elect, if that was possible (Matthew 24:23-24). But it is not possible, for Christ upholds His elect.

Be settled even in times of war or threats of war (Matthew 24:6). The City of God is distinct from man's city and will survive regardless of what happens in politics or in war. We are neither to be unduly encouraged by political events nor unduly frightened by them. Instead, stand firm to the end.

You should not spend your time wondering about the specific moment of Jesus' return. You should be asking yourself if you are ready, whenever it might occur.

Revelation 12:1-10

1. And there appeared a great wonder in heaven; a woman clothed with the sun, and the moon under her feet, and upon her head a crown of twelve stars:

2. And she being with child cried, travailing in birth, and pained to be delivered.

3. And there appeared another wonder in heaven; and behold a great red dragon, having seven heads and ten horns, and seven crowns upon his heads.

4. And his tail drew the third part of the stars of heaven, and did cast them to the earth: and the dragon stood before the woman which was ready to be delivered, for to devour her child as soon as it was born.

5. And she brought forth a man child, who was to rule all nations with a rod of iron: and her child was caught up unto God, and to his throne.

6. And the woman fled into the wilderness, where she hath a place prepared of God, that they should feed her there a thousand two hundred and threescore days.

7. And there was war in heaven: Michael and his angels fought against the dragon; and the dragon fought and his angels,

8. And prevailed not; neither was their place found any more in heaven.

9. And the great dragon was cast out, that old serpent, called the Devil, and Satan, which deceiveth the whole world: he was cast out into the earth, and his angels were cast out with him.

10. And I heard a loud voice saying in heaven, Now is come salvation, and strength, and the kingdom of our God, and the power of his Christ: for the accuser of our brethren is cast down, which accused them before our God day and night.

CHAPTER 3

The Woman, Dragon, and Male Child

A Repulsive Scene

What an awful scene we find in Revelation 12. It reminds us of how the old serpent tried to devour Adam and Eve in Paradise. How repulsive, ugly, and evil it is to see the Devil trying to destroy the innocent man child of the woman! John sees a vision, in which a great red dragon – the Devil – tries to devour the Christ child.

In this vision, the Dragon does not actually devour the man child, but in Zambia, a python did in fact accomplish its intent. ABC News reported that a Python swallowed a Zambian newborn. The title of the story was: "Barely Born: Python Swallows Zambian Newborn." The story followed:

> "A python swallowed a baby minutes after it was born near the central Zambian town of Serenje, state television reported today. Heavily pregnant Joyce Mibenge was on her way to plough fields a mile from her home when she went into labor, ZNBC reported. Halfway home, she was overwhelmed by labor pains

and retreated into a nearby bush to rest. She gave birth there on her own. After a few moments when she had recovered enough to hold her baby she saw a happy python licking the legs of the baby with the rest already swallowed," ZNBC said. The traumatized Mibenge pulled herself to her feet, fled to her home and raised the alarm, but searching villagers were unable to find the snake. She didn't even know whether she had had a boy or girl.

What a terrible story! In Revelation 12, we read of a dragon-like serpent whose eyes are focused on a woman in delivery. Instead of being devoured, the child is caught up to Heaven and soon judges the serpent with a rod of iron.

Revelation 12 is a panoramic view of the incarnation of our Lord Jesus Christ and its results. The conflict between the church and the world is but the outward manifestation of the war between God and Satan.

John beholds "a great sign" in Heaven. By saying this, John indicates that we must not expect a literal description of something real, but symbolism. The first wonder or sign is a woman. John sees a beautiful, glorious, pregnant woman.

The woman is so important that even the heavenly bodies of light must serve her, adding to her splendor. The sun, in all its glory of light, is her clothing. The moon is under her feet, for she exercises dominion. She wears on her head a crown of twelve stars. Although she is glorious, she has not reached the purpose of her existence and is not perfectly happy and blessed. She is great with child. She is suffering the pains of childbirth.

The Identity of the Woman

Who is the woman? She is the church of God. Her crown of twelve stars reminds us of the eleven stars that Joseph saw in his dream. Twelve is the number of the church. She is not the Virgin Mary, for later she is pictured as having many children.

The church is great with child due to the fact that she has conceived in the mother promise. Because of the power of the promise, she is pregnant throughout the Old Testament. The Messiah is in the womb of the church.

The pregnant woman culminates in a virgin who is impregnated by the power of the Holy Spirit. In the Old Testament, the Church lived continually in the expectation that the Messiah would be born from her. Enoch prophesied of the Messiah coming for judgment. Abraham longed to see His day. Jacob foretold Christ. Moses spoke of the coming of the great Prophet. Isaiah prophesied of the Messiah's royal government. Simeon did not want to die before seeing the Hope of Israel.

This vision pictures the entire Old Testament church travailing in pain and longing and expecting to bring forth the man child.

At first glance, the thought that the church is glorious may seem farfetched. The church on earth seems far from glorious. The church in the Old Testament was small, mostly Jewish, and often beset by sin and idolatry. In the church today, worldliness, materialism, small numbers, and false doctrine seem to abound on every side.

But the church is essentially glorious as the elect people of God, purchased by Christ, and as the dwelling place of the Holy Spirit.

The Great Red Dragon

The second sign is a great red dragon. A dragon in Scripture seems to indicate not one of God's own created animals in its natural appearance, but rather a monster. A monster departs considerably from the usual size and shape of an animal. God never made a snake with seven heads! The main feature of this monster is that of a serpent.

He is called "the old serpent" (Revelation 12:9). Imagine a winged serpent with crested head and destructive claws. Envision seven snake heads coming from one thick body. The monster is a great *red* dragon. Red is a picture of blood, war, and destruction. So immense in size is this dragon that its mammoth tail, furiously lashing across the sky, sweeps away one-third of the stars of heaven.

He has seven heads and ten crowns. Seven is the number of the covenant. The seven heads symbolize that the Devil tries to ape the church. Do not be deceived.

His ten crowns are not real, either. They are not made in Heaven. They are counterfeit. Wicked men at the instigation of the Devil seize power, although they do not have the right to rule. They have no right to reign in God's world. But God is sovereign over this illicit seizure of power. The ten crowns denote a certain measure of authority and power that God allots to the Devil by His decree. God ordains that wicked men should reign.

The identity of the great red dragon is revealed. We are told: "And the great dragon was cast out, that old serpent, called 'the Devil,' and Satan, which deceiveth the whole world" (Revelation 12:9). Why is the Devil pictured like this? God did not make him a monster. God made him a glorious archangel. But he made himself into a monster through his rebellion. He is the great deceiver, the subtle snake. He was a murderer from the beginning as his redness implies.

The Incarnation

The incarnation of Christ is the great wonder John beheld. The woman stands in her glory, but also in her helplessness, as the dragon stands before her. With intent watchfulness and devilish purpose, the dragon studies her every movement. The man child is evidently of great importance to him. He waits, ready to devour the newborn baby.

Here we see the beastliness of the Devil! How repulsive it is to watch a dragon try to devour God's innocent Son incarnate!

The Devil lives in the expectation of the birth of this man child. He was right there when God gave the mother promise in Genesis 3:15. In fact, the promise was given in the form of a challenge to the Devil.

Throughout the Old Testament, the Devil had been trying to destroy the possibility of this man child being born. Cain killed Abel. The Devil encouraged intermarriage before the Flood. He inspired Pharaoh who tried to kill Israel's baby boys.

Then the child is born. The scene is Bethlehem. The Devil lunges for Him. "Be sure," King Herod says to the magi, "to tell me as soon as you find the child, that I may also come and worship Him" (Matthew 2:8). But Herod failed to kill the newborn king. His failure was the Dragon's failure.

The Devil failed again in the wilderness temptations. He failed in Gethsemane. The cross turned out to be his Waterloo.

In this vision, John sees the ascension of Jesus to the right hand of God: "And her child was caught up unto God, and to his throne" (Revelation 12:5).

Misinterpretations of Pre-millennialists

Pre-millennialists take this event to be something that will happen only at the end of the world. They interpret the man child being caught up to God to teach the doctrine of a secret rapture! One pre-millennialist, Ray Stedman, says:

> But – and here is where it gets a bit tricky – there is an aspect of our Lord which found deliverance from danger by being snatched away into Heaven. How many of you have guessed what it is? It is the church, of

course...The church and the Lord are together the body of Christ. So the whole history of the church is involved here, including the rapture. It is interesting that the term used here for the child is that he was snatched up to God. That is the very term that is used for the rapture of the church. It is the Great Snatch!...the Great Snatch, the rapture of the church, to occur before the dragon begins his persecuting work.

Pre-millennialists transform the man child into the whole church. But we know from Psalm 2:9 that the child is the Christ and is presented as the One "who is to rule the nations with a rod of iron." Furthermore, the name "the son (or seed) of a woman" is used elsewhere to indicate the Christ (Genesis 3:15, Galatians 4:4). The child is the Christ-child who ascended victoriously into Heaven. The result is a battle in Heaven that brings great joy to the saints.

The Timing of the War

The Apostle John records a war in Heaven:

And there was war in heaven: Michael and his angels fought against the dragon; and the dragon fought and his angels, And prevailed not; neither was their place found any more in heaven (Revelation 12:7-8).

We could call this war the Ascension Day War. Some think this battle in heaven occurred before Satan entered Paradise to tempt Adam and Eve. Some argue that this war happened throughout the entire Old Testament. Others think that this war is still in the future, immediately following a rapture (pre-millennialist interpretation). However, the Scriptures clearly teach that the timing was Ascension Day.

38

This Ascension Day War is not a picture of the battle that occurred throughout all the ages, ever since Satan deceived one-third of the angels into rebelling against God. In this war, the elect angels, under Michael, take the offensive. They clearly have been given the command to attack to achieve a specific victory.

If we follow the vision, we discover that John sees this war in heaven after he sees Christ symbolically being born. He saw a woman who gave birth to a child. Satan, pictured like a great red dragon, stood ready to seize the baby. The man child is born who is the Messiah, for he "was to rule all nations with a rod of iron." Then comes the critical statement: "And her child was caught up unto God, and to his throne" (Revelation 12:5b). This is a reference to the ascension and exaltation of Jesus Christ. Christ, having endured the assaults of the Devil, is now in His resurrected body exalted to God's right hand. Therefore, this is a vision of Ascension Day.

The holy angels are given a command to fight and hurl their angelic enemies out of Heaven. The object of this warfare was to empty Heaven of devils.

Until this point, Satan had taken advantage of the open door into Heaven to accuse the saints before God. In the Old Testament, we find the devils could go into Heaven. An evil spirit could volunteer to deceive the King of Israel. Satan could come on a certain day before the throne of God and be challenged over the faithfulness of godly Job. The accuser's legal argument was that the Old Testament saints did not deserve to be in Heaven because no one had paid for their sins. Satan claimed that they were guilty and worthy of damnation.

It is true that God in His eternal counsel already saw Jesus Christ as sacrificed for His people. But historically, Christ had not yet come. Satan had hoped somehow to avoid the triumph of the seed of the woman.

But now Christ has come. The truth that His people are justified cannot be contradicted by the Devil because Jesus is in Heaven to make intercession for His people. The wounds in His hands and feet are evidence that He has redeemed His elect. Abraham, Isaac, and Jacob have the right to live in Paradise. Christ paid for their sins. Christ has pulled the carpet out from under the objections of the accuser of the brethren.

A Literal Battle in Heaven

The Ascension Day War was a literal battle. This battle was fought by Michael the archangel and the elect angels against Satan and the Devils. Strangely, Michael has been identified as Jesus. But in Scripture, he is identified as an archangel (Jude 9). His name means, "who is like God." This name certainly could not apply to Christ, since Christ is not merely like God, but is God!

In Scripture, we find that Michael fights on behalf of God's people. In Jude, we learn that he did not allow Satan to take Moses' body. In Daniel, we find that Michael helped an angel who was trying to get to Daniel. Daniel identifies the archangel as "the great prince which standeth for the children of thy people" (Daniel 12:1).

Two generals and two armies oppose each other. The opposing general claimed that he was like God. The enemy is identified as "the great dragon," "that old serpent, called the Devil, and Satan, which deceiveth the whole world" (Revelation 12:9).

Michael and the holy angels went on the offensive. This is a spiritual battle fought not with swords, but spiritual weapons – weapons of intellect and the Word of God. When Michael the Archangel fought with Satan, he used a prayer to defeat Satan: "The Lord rebuke thee" (Jude 9).

Michael and the angels must have shouted at Satan and the devils that the Kingdom of Christ has come! Christ was being enthroned! Myriads of angels welcomed the crucified, resurrected, and now ascended Lord Jesus into Heaven. The truth of the ascension shouted in the ears of the devils meant the end of scurrilous charges against the elect.

The Outcome of the Battle

The saints in Heaven celebrate the reign of Jesus Christ: "Now is come salvation, and strength, and the kingdom of our God " (Revelation 12:10).

The devils were defeated! Heaven was emptied of devils. While there were some long faces on earth on Ascension Day, such was not the case in Heaven.

In his vision, John sees a massive celebration in Heaven. Saints in Heaven celebrate that the accuser is cast out.

By His cross, Jesus Christ has taken away all of the Devil's ammunition. In the great exchange, Jesus Christ took all of our unrighteousness upon Himself. He suffered and paid for our sins. Through faith in Jesus Christ, His righteousness is imputed to elect believers.

No longer can Satan claim that the inhabitants of Heaven do not deserve to be there. The door of Heaven is now shut to that great red dragon. Slandering the church triumphant in Paradise itself is no longer tolerated. "Who shall lay any thing to the charge of God's elect? It is God that justifieth" (Romans 8:33).

Because of His defeat, Satan is filled with wrath. This results in further warfare. Now, the Devil directs all his efforts toward the persecution and destruction of the church militant on earth. He constantly brings accusations against believers. He tries to get us to think that we cannot be right with God because of our sins.

He knows that his time is short. Listen to the warning for the church: "Woe to the inhabiters of the earth and of the sea! For the Devil is come down unto you, having great wrath, because he knoweth that he hath but a short time" (Revelation 12:12b).

The One Church of All Ages

John then sees the dragon attack the church of Jesus Christ. This vision connects the church in the Old Testament and the church in the New Testament. They are one.

First, we see the Old Testament church pregnant with Christ. Later, she is also said to have "seed" (Revelation 12:17). She is the mother of the New Testament church! This is important. It implies that the church in all ages is one. In the Old Testament, this same woman is pregnant with Christ. Now in the New Testament, she is the same woman – but now her children, who, according to verse 17, "keep the commandments of God, and have the testimony of Jesus Christ," include both Jews and Gentiles.

You should love the church as your spiritual mother. She exists for your spiritual care and nourishment. The church is the institute church as she submits to the reign of Jesus Christ, confesses the truth of the gospel, rightly administers the sacraments, and carries out Christian discipline. Through the preaching of the Word and administration of the sacraments, we are all strengthened.

Safety in Spiritual Separation

God protects the church by separating her from the sinful world.

> And to the woman were given two wings of a great eagle, that she might fly into the wilderness, into her place, where she is nourished for a time, and times, and half a time, from the face of the serpent (Revelation 12:14).

The church is safe as she lives in spiritual separation from the sinful world.

Just like the Israelites were literally led out of the sinful world (typified by Egypt) into the wilderness where they could worship God in separation, so the church is kept spiritually separate. In her holiness, there is strength! God protects His people by nourishing them with the manna of the Word.

The serpent sends a flood out of his mouth: "And the serpent cast out of his mouth water as a flood after the woman, that he might cause her to be carried away of the flood" (Revelation 12:15). Note that the serpent does not try to drown the woman, but to float her out of her place of security and separation in the wilderness.

In the same way, Satan tries to engulf and compromise the church by a stream of lies. He uses Joseph Smith and false revelations in a supposed book of Mormon, as well as philosophical falsehoods like those of Immanuel Kant, who claimed that humans could not know anything about the "noumena," God, or spiritual things. He uses political utopias like communism, as well as quasi-scientific dogmas like Darwinism to swallow up the church.

He tries to get the church to conform to the world. The Devil realizes that in the church's isolation from the world lies her strength. He wants her to become like the world, so he uses delusions, lies, heresies, sinful lusts, Mammon, and worldliness.

However, Satan fails to destroy the church institute: "And the earth helped the woman, and the earth opened her mouth, and swallowed up the flood which the dragon cast out of his mouth" (Revelation 12:16).

Always, God preserves His church. God does not allow the true church to be fooled.

Pursued as Individual Christians

The Devil also goes after individual believers:

> And the dragon was wroth with the woman, and went
> to make war with the remnant of her seed, which keep
> the commandments of God, and have the testimony of
> Jesus Christ (Revelation 12:17).

When the Devil fails to destroy the Church, he turns on
individual believers. He can make life hard for you. The
Devil hates us Christians and he summons his subordinates
to attack us. Satan uses wicked men as tools to attack our
reputation. Devils even find a point of contact in the
imperfect hearts of fellow Christians so that they even use
sinning fellow Christians to try to destroy us.

Protected by Victorious Angels

There is an ancient prediction in the last chapter of the
book of Daniel:

> And at that time shall Michael stand up, the great
> prince which standeth for the children of thy people:
> and there shall be a time of trouble, such as never was
> since there was a nation even to that same time: and at
> that time thy people shall be delivered, every one that
> shall be found written in the book (Daniel 12:1).

We are not only safe with God as our mighty fortress, but
millions of angels, in the company of Michael, protect us. It is
marvelous that we have such mighty angels who guard us.
They surround us with angelic wings. We little understand
how much the holy angels love us and how mightily they
battle on our behalf.

3. And I will give power unto my two witnesses, and they shall prophesy a thousand two hundred and threescore days, clothed in sackcloth.

4. These are the two olive trees, and the two candlesticks standing before the God of the earth.

5. And if any man will hurt them, fire proceedeth out of their mouth, and devoureth their enemies: and if any man will hurt them, he must in this manner be killed.

6. These have power to shut heaven, that it rain not in the days of their prophecy: and have power over waters to turn them to blood, and to smite the earth with all plagues, as often as they will.

7. And when they shall have finished their testimony, the beast that ascendeth out of the bottomless pit shall make war against them, and shall overcome them, and kill them.

8. And their dead bodies shall lie in the street of the great city, which spiritually is called Sodom and Egypt, where also our Lord was crucified.

9. And they of the people and kindreds and tongues and nations shall see their dead bodies three days and an half, and shall not suffer their dead bodies to be put in graves.

10. And they that dwell upon the earth shall rejoice over them, and make merry, and shall send gifts one to another; because these two prophets tormented them that dwelt on the earth.

11. And after three days and an half the Spirit of life from God entered into them, and they stood upon their feet; and great fear fell upon them which saw them.

12. And they heard a great voice from heaven saying unto them, Come up hither. And they ascended up to heaven in a cloud; and their enemies beheld them.

13. And the same hour was there a great earthquake, and the tenth part of the city fell, and in the earthquake were slain of men seven thousand: and the remnant were affrighted, and gave glory to the God of heaven.

14. The second woe is past; and, behold, the third woe cometh quickly.

CHAPTER 4

The Two Witnesses

Do you identify yourself with the two witnesses prophesied of in Revelation 11? Are you clothed in sackcloth as you realize your sinfulness? Do you ask God for spiritual strength to be like these witnesses?

Who are these famous two witnesses? This is an important question that also determines the answer to other questions about their calling and victory. We must admit that this is one of the most difficult questions in the book of Revelation. But we also confess that by interpreting Scripture with Scripture, the Holy Spirit can help us answer this hard question.

Different ministers and commentators have given numerous answers to this question. Dr. Martyn Lloyd-Jones said that they symbolized the Law and Gospel. Some Reformers thought that they were a picture of the Old and New Testaments.

Some church fathers and most pre-millennialists believe the witnesses are two famous Old Testament patriarchs, Enoch and Elijah. At the end of the Old Testament, in Malachi 4:5-6, prophecy speaks about how God would send Elijah. Jewish tradition said that Enoch would also return. Enoch and Elijah are identified as the two witnesses because they both witnessed in times of apostasy, both were preachers of repentance and judgment, and both escaped death.

In the *Left Behind* series, Tim LaHaye and Jerry Jenkins portray the two witnesses as Moses and Elijah. For dramatic purposes, they reinstate their Hebrew names, giving Moses the Hebrew sounding "Moishe," for example. These pre-millennial novelists try to take the numbers in Revelation as literal, not symbolic. Yet they take the three and one half *days* referenced in Revelation 11:9 to be three and a half literal *years*. Notice the discrepancy. Although they claim to take symbolic numbers literally, they actually do not interpret them literally.

In their novel, they dramatically picture Moses and Elijah returning to earth by the Wailing Wall in Jerusalem. There, they preach with powerful voices and everybody is able to hear and understand them.

The drama grows as the novelists picture snipers and assassins coming to Jerusalem to kill them and end their witness. When snipers approach, whether part of the Global Government or anyone who takes advantage of a license to kill, the assassins are destroyed by fire. Flames burst from the mouths of the witnesses and incinerate the assassins, melting their machine guns and blackening their flesh. Certainly, it is attractive and dramatic to interpret the two witnesses to be Moses and Elijah, who return to earth to incinerate United Nations soldiers!

We must not limit the interpretation of the two witnesses to the Old Testament. Instead, we should understand that they are types.

Let us try to understand whom these witnesses represent. First, note that the witnesses are pictured in universal features. They have universal influence. They are the objects of universal hatred. Only if we understand them in a different sense will we understand and appreciate what this passage teaches about them. I cannot imagine that God, who glorified Moses and Elijah, would allow them to return to this sinful world and suffer death. Why should Moses, who already died, be killed again?

It is true that Malachi prophesied of the coming of Elijah before the great and dreadful day of the Lord. But Jesus shows us that was not meant to be taken literally (Matthew 17:10-13, Matthew 11:14). The idea is that someone would come in the spirit and power of Elijah. That man was John the Baptist. John the Baptist was Elijah.

The Bible never predicts Moses and Elijah would literally return. In Revelation 11:4, we have a clue to the identity of these witnesses: "These are the two olive trees, and the two candlesticks standing before the God of the earth." The reference is clearly to Zechariah 4:11-14. In Zechariah 4:11, the prophet asks: "What are these two olive trees upon the right side of the candlestick and upon the left side thereof?" The answer is: "These are the two anointed ones, that stand before the Lord of the whole earth" (Zechariah 4:14).

The identity of the two olive trees and the candlestick in Zechariah 4:11 is the same as that of the two witnesses in Revelation 11:3!

In the context of Zechariah chapter 4, the Prophet Zechariah saw a vision of seven lamp stands on a single stand. Pipes or tubes attached to each of the lamps and ran up to a golden bowl filled with oil. The golden bowl had pipes running up to two olive trees. So, the olive trees provided the bowl with oil, which in turn provided oil for the lamps to burn.

God gives the general meaning of this vision to Zerubbabel: "Not by might, nor by power, but by my Spirit, saith the Lord" (Zechariah 4:6). After the return from

Babylon, Zerubbabel was charged with rebuilding the temple. God tells him that only by the power of the Spirit will this occur. Although God uses human instruments, nevertheless the completion of the work depends on the Holy Spirit.

The lamp stands are symbolic of the people of God shining as witnesses. In Revelation 1, we find the same symbolism with Christ walking in the midst of seven golden lamp stands. The golden lamp stands symbolize the true church of God as it is manifested in a specific geographic locality. The true church is to shine like a lamp.

But who are the two olive trees? Zechariah 4:14 tells us they are the two anointed ones, standing before the Lord of the whole earth. First, they are servants of God. Second, they are anointed, officially called and ordained. That they are anointed implies they possess a special office. The Holy Spirit equips them to carry out their office. Most commentators admit that they are Zerubbabel, the governor, and Jeshua, the high priest.

Office bearers are an important means by which God gives grace to His people so they can shine as lights. So, the olive trees represent the ordained and called office bearers of God--elders, deacons, and ministers. God uses office-bearers as a conduit to equip the saints so that they can shine as bright lights.

In light of Zechariah, the identity of the two witnesses becomes clear. They are not only the two olive trees, nor only the two candlesticks; they are both! The olive trees and candlesticks cannot be separated. They belong together.

Together, the church and office bearers of the New Testament are the two witnesses. Just as God had two witnesses in the Old Testament, so He does today. The number two is used because it is symbolic of how two witnesses are needed for a man to be found guilty in a court of law.

Office bearers and all the members of the church are able to witness "not by might, nor by power," but only by the power of the Spirit of Christ. Christ's anointing enables them to testify about Jesus in the last days.

In the early verses of Revelation 11, an angel gives John a reed and tells him to measure the temple, but not the outer court of the Gentiles. To be counted or measured in the book of Revelation is often a picture of being set apart, distinguished, or separated. Those who are not counted are members of the apostate or false church. The outer court is a picture of false Christianity, which will grow powerful.

The church and her office bearers are to witness about the gospel of Jesus Christ and the truth of the gospel. Moses, Elijah, and Jeremiah did this during difficult days in the Old Testament. In the New Testament, the apostles were almost all martyrs. Prior to the reformation, John Huss was a faithful witness. Following the reformation, many Reformed believers in the Netherlands and France were faithful witnesses and martyrs.

Today, the church must let her light shine boldly and fearlessly. Herman Hoeksema emphasizes that the church is to witness in word and deed. Speaking of the two anointed ones and writing of what applies to the church, Hoeksema says:

> And that they stand before the Lord of the whole earth also implies that they are especially the ones that are ready to serve the Lord before the whole world with their testimony in word and deed.

Regardless of what false Christians or the world may say, we must witness and do what is right.

We must witness about the issues that are under the fiercest attack. If you are protecting many areas of the walls of Zion, but not the section under attack, you are a faulty defender. In the 21st Century, this means Christians must defend the truth about the institution of marriage.

An important part of your witnessing is calling men to repentance. That is the implication of the sackcloth worn by the two witnesses (Revelation 11:3). Sackcloth was rough, heavy cloth worn in ancient times as a symbol of mourning, distress, or grief. Jacob wore sackcloth after he thought Joseph was dead. David ordered the Israelites to wear sackcloth after Abner's murder. Isaiah and Daniel also wore sackcloth. We must witness about the great need for members of the false church and unbelievers to repent in dust and ashes.

We must witness to the ends of the earth. The church must be a great missionary institution at home and abroad. She must proclaim Christ where He has never been heard. We must witness to our families, our neighbors, and hurting people.

We must battle with the Word and by prayer. The witnesses send fire out of their mouths to destroy their enemies:

> And if any man will hurt them, fire proceedeth out of their mouth, and devoureth their enemies: and if any man will hurt them, he must in this manner be killed (Revelation 11:5).

During Jesus time on earth, some Samaritans made James and John angry; they wanted Jesus to call down fire from Heaven like Elijah. In Jesus' rebuke, He clearly taught that New Testament believers do not physically kill or wound. They fight with spiritual weapons. They love. They witness.

They show mercy. They bless those who curse them. They do good to those who do evil to them.

John sees fire come out of the mouths of the witnesses to destroy their enemies. John records specifically that the fire comes not from heaven, but out of the mouths of the witnesses (Revelation 11:5). We look to Jeremiah 5:14 in order to discover the meaning of this fire proceeding out of the mouth of the church:

> Wherefore thus saith the LORD God of hosts, Because ye speak this word, behold, I will make my words in thy mouth fire, and this people wood, and it shall devour them (Jeremiah 5:14).

At this time, the Israelites wanted to kill Jeremiah, but God would protect him and make His Word like a fire in the prophet's mouth. Before the power of the Word, the wicked would not be able to stand. The wicked are nothing but flammable wood. They are easily rebuked, judged, and proved wrong. The weapon of the Word of God is an important defensive weapon. We can defend the truth easily and shame the error.

What is prophesied is that nothing will be able to stop the witness of the church. Heresy will not silence us! Persecution will not silence us - not yet, anyway! The gates of Hell cannot prevail against this mighty missionary force.

We can use prayer to send plagues on this wicked world:

> "These have power to shut heaven, that it rain not in the days of their prophecy; and have power over waters to turn them to blood, and to smite the earth with all plagues, as often as they will" (Revelation 11:6).

A remarkable power is invested in us. The church has the power to cause famine. Did you know that? The reference here is clearly to Elijah and Moses. God used Moses to turn the Nile into blood and other plagues. Elijah kneeled down in the wilderness of Gilead and prayed that it would not rain, and it did not for three and a half years.

We cannot just spiritualize this to refer to Christian discipline. Nor must we take this too literally as if we will actually turn water into blood. But the reference clearly is to our ability to pray that God would send terrible judgments on the wicked world and the apostate church.

It is true that the church is not always aware of this awesome power. God expects us to pray imprecatory prayers as the evil days at the end approach. Living in the last days, we should be conscious of this calling. We can pray down judgment upon governments like the communist one in China that is officially anti-Christian. But especially the church in the last days will pray down judgments upon the Antichristian world. And in heaven, God will hear. He will send great judgments in answer to the prayers of His witnesses.

The Victory of the Witnesses

This vision implies that terrible days lay ahead for the witnessing church: "And when they shall have finished their testimony, the beast that ascendeth out of the bottomless pit shall make war against them, and shall overcome them, and kill them" (Revelation 11:7).

For the first time, we meet the Antichrist in Revelation in Revelation 11:7. We will soon look at this monstrous man in greater detail. The time will have arrived when the church on earth has finished her public testimony. The gospel will have been brought to the nations.

The Antichrist kills the two witnesses. This is symbolic of him destroying the public witness of the church. She will be like the church in Afghanistan. If she exists at all, it will only be underground. Church buildings will be closed to public worship.

Antichrist will murder many saints. He will make sport of the fact that Christianity has been wiped off the face of the earth. The Antichrist will desecrate the two witnesses by exposing the bodies of his enemy's dead bodies on the streets of Jerusalem for three days. The whole world will party! There will be a real run on alcohol! The wicked will send gifts and party because the church, who tormented them by her witness about God's holiness and the judgment to come, will have fallen silent.

Notice that this is done in the city of Jerusalem, which is here a picture of the false church. The false church, like the Roman Catholic Church and the liberal mainline Methodist and Presbyterian Churches, is called "Sodom and Gomorrah." Many mainline churches today are already like Sodom in their defense of ordaining actively homosexual ministers. This city is also described as "where also our Lord was crucified" (Revelation 11:8).

But after three days, a short time, the church is pictured as being resurrected. The antichristian world will be horrified to see the church revived. "And they heard a great voice from heaven saying unto them, Come up hither. And they ascended up to heaven in a cloud; and their enemies beheld them" (Revelation 11:12).

It is at this point that Herman Hoeksema makes a mistake in his interpretation. While Hoeksema has many good insights into the interpretation of the book of Revelation in his book, *Behold, He Cometh*, he makes a serious mistake at this point. The Dutch American theologian teaches that before the end, the church will be taken out of the earth. Hoeksema writes:

> In other words, before the time of the end, while the Antichrist and the Gog and Magog are still on earth, the church, shall be taken away from her shame and persecution and terrible suffering. The living saints shall be changed. Those that have died shall be raised. And the church of Christ shall be glorified.

This cannot be true, since we know from Scripture that when Christ returns, He will find believers in the world. For example, Jesus says about judgment day, "And he shall send his angels with a great sound of a trumpet, and they shall gather together his elect from the four winds, from one end of heaven to the other" (Matthew 24:31).

In the vision in Revelation 11, John immediately sees God unleashing furious judgments upon Jerusalem:

> And the same hour was there a great earthquake, and the tenth part of the city fell, and in the earthquake were slain of men seven thousand: the remnant were affrighted, and gave glory to the God of heaven (Revelation 11:13).

A tenth is symbolic of the whole. The power and dominion of the Antichrist is taken away.

Revelation 20:1-10

1. And I saw an angel come down from heaven, having the key of the bottomless pit and a great chain in his hand.

2. And he laid hold on the dragon, that old serpent, which is the Devil, and Satan, and bound him a thousand years,

3. And cast him into the bottomless pit, and shut him up, and set a seal upon him, that he should deceive the nations no more, till the thousand years should be fulfilled: and after that he must be loosed a little season.

4. And I saw thrones, and they sat upon them, and judgment was given unto them: and I saw the souls of them that were beheaded for the witness of Jesus, and for the word of God, and which had not worshipped the beast, neither his image, neither had received his mark upon their foreheads, or in their hands; and they lived and reigned with Christ a thousand years.

5. But the rest of the dead lived not again until the thousand years were finished. This is the first resurrection.

6. Blessed and holy is he that hath part in the first resurrection: on such the second death hath no power, but they shall be priests of God and of Christ, and shall reign with him a thousand years.

7. And when the thousand years are expired, Satan shall be loosed out of his prison,

8. And shall go out to deceive the nations which are in the four quarters of the earth, Gog and Magog, to gather them together to battle: the number of whom is as the sand of the sea.

9. And they went up on the breadth of the earth, and compassed the camp of the saints about, and the beloved city: and fire came down from God out of heaven, and devoured them.

10. And the devil that deceived them was cast into the lake of fire and brimstone, where the beast and the false prophet are, and shall be tormented day and night for ever and ever.

CHAPTER 5

The Millennium

In the vision the Apostle John sees in Revelation 20, God reveals the role Satan's imprisonment, release, defeat, and damnation will play at the end of human history.

Revelation 20 is one of the most controversial passages in the New Testament. Yet, the meaning of the passage is clear and straightforward. The application is easy to understand.

John saw the Devil bound for a millennium – a thousand years. This millennium is interpreted three ways. First, the pre-millennialists believe Christ will return to reign on earth prior to a literal thousand-year reign in Jerusalem.

Second, the post-millennialists believe Christ will return following a thousand-year period of world Christianization. Some post-millennialists do not take the thousand-year period literally, but talk as if the millennium could be thousands of years during which the gospel advances.

Third, the Reformers and the church father Augustine take the position of a-millennialism. The letter "a" at the beginning means "not." Therefore, a-millennialism means that this millennium is not to be taken literally, but symbolically. There will be no literal thousand-year period during which Jesus reigns on a fallen planet Earth.

We believe this latter position is true. We shall see that the number 1,000 is symbolic of Christ's present reign with the saints in Heaven from the time of His ascension to the time of the end.

In many American churches, pre-millennialism is regarded as a test of orthodoxy. Throughout the twentieth century, professors at Wheaton College needed to sign a pledge declaring they were pre-millennialists. Pre-millennialism is the dominant view held by American fundamentalists and evangelicals.

Pre-millennialists believe that when John speaks of a thousand years, he means a literal one thousand years. They believe that when John speaks of the binding of Satan, which begins the thousand years, he must be referring to a time after Jesus returns for a second time. The first return is at the rapture, while the second return is to smash the Antichrist. It is the binding of Satan that guarantees a thousand years of peace on earth.

Pre-millennialists argue that Revelation 20 chronologically follows Revelation 19. They create several serious theological problems that cannot be easily dismissed. First, where, in this passage, does John describe universal peace on earth? Second, where does John speak of Jesus Christ ruling from the city of Jerusalem over the inhabitants of the earth? Third, where does John ever teach or imply that *resurrected* believers live on the earth with unregenerate sinners?

The historic Protestant position, taught by all the Reformers, is a-millennialism. Instead of holding to the "a" meaning not or no, it is better to understand this as a *present* millennium.

The millennium refers to the present reign of Jesus Christ in heaven. The thousand years is a symbolic reference to the entire period between Christ's first coming and His second coming. At the end of the millennium, Satan will be allowed to rally the nations against the church. The Antichrist will seize power and persecute the church. Satan, through the Antichrist, will be able to wipe out the public witness of the church. After a short while, Christ will return to destroy His enemies. He will establish the New Heaven and the New Earth.

Revelation 20 does not follow after the events described in Revelation 19 in any chronological sense. Revelation 20 contains another vision, which like the others describes the entire period of time between the first coming and the second coming of Jesus. It does so from yet a different theological camera angle, this time depicting the fate of the dragon.

In chapter 19, we see the end times from the camera perspective of the rebellion and destruction of the Antichrist and the false prophet. God directs our full attention to Satan's imprisonment, release, defeat, and damnation. Revelation 19 depicts the destruction of Christ's enemies. The birds of prey feast upon the remains of all men, great and small. The beast and the false prophet are thrown into the Lake of Fire.

It follows that in Revelation 20 we find a retelling of the final judgment from yet another perspective. It is a description of this present age, viewed from the perspective of the final fate of the dragon. The binding of the Devil is a symbolic act.

The Dragon Arrested!

The Apostle John, while on the island of Patmos, envisions an amazing scene. A mighty angel is sent out with an arrest warrant. The angel takes a mighty chain and handcuffs and binds Satan. He then throws the Devil into prison – the abyss. He turns the key in the lock, thereby locking the dragon in his prison.

John never intends us to understand symbolic events as literal. How can an angel bind a spiritual being (Satan) with a real chain? An angelic spirit cannot be manacled with a chain, but a spirit can be constrained by a divine command. A "key" signifies authority to open or close. God ordains that Satan be unable to deceive the nations in such a way that would make the worldwide spread of the gospel impossible during the New Testament age.

Satan is bound in the abyss for a specified time (1,000 years). Numbers are used symbolically throughout Revelation. In Scripture, we often find the number ten denotes the idea of completeness or fullness. There were ten plagues upon Egypt, which symbolized the fullness of God's wrath. There are Ten Commandments, expressing the fullness of God's ethical will for men. One thousand is the third power of ten, and is therefore, symbolic of a long period of time that is complete.

Jesus never teaches a thousand-year reign with the saints on earth. The binding of the Devil is for a specific purpose (so that Satan is prevented from deceiving the nations). This raises an important question: Is this imprisonment of Satan absolute or partial?

Pre-millennialists claim the fact that Satan is bound with a chain and locked up in the abyss means he is completely helpless; therefore, during the millennium, the nations all submit to Jesus Christ.

Scripture actually teaches that this restraint is partial and with a view to a certain purpose. The text does not teach that all of the devils are bound. Even if Satan was completely helpless, all of his demons could be hard at work. The text teaches that Satan is bound "that he should deceive the nations no more" (Revelation 20:3). In Revelation 20:8, we are informed that when Satan is freed, he is able to deceive the nations, Gog and Magog, to gather them to battle.

This establishes first that the binding of Satan is limited to certain nations who are called Gog and Magog. Second, his confinement prevents him from deceiving these nations. Third, Satan is unable to gather these nations for battle against Christians to destroy their public witness.

Therefore, the binding of Satan does not mean that his evil activities completely cease during the thousand years. In fact, John has already told us in Revelation 12:12 that Satan is filled with fury because his time is short. Like a wounded animal sure to die, Satan is more of a threat than ever. He is more dangerous now than when he had free access to Heaven. He prowls like a roaring lion. You can put a vicious dog on a chain, but you do not want to get within the radius of the chain or you will get mauled! Think of Al Capone, a mobster who governed his kingdom – the Chicago underground – from behind bars when necessary.

John's point is not that Satan ceases all activity during the thousand years, but that Satan is prevented from deceiving the nations so as to organize them against the church. Therefore, in Revelation 20, God reminds a suffering and persecuted church that Satan is under God's sovereign control. Satan is very securely bound.

We see the result of this binding in world missions. The Devil has been unable to stop the advance of Christ's gospel across the globe. The nations of the world have received the glad tidings.

Satan is bound like a gang leader packed off to a maximum security prison to isolate him from his gang. In the State of Illinois, leaders of threat groups once were sent to a super max prison in southern Illinois. But the reality is that a gang leader in the super max prison could still be a threat. He would find ways to communicate with his underlings. He would still actively scheme and try to carry out his nefarious plans in spite of the limitations imposed on him.

So it is with Satan during the New Testament era. He is chained, yet dangerous. He is bound, yet free to lead the rebellion within the bounds imposed upon him by Christ.

The Glorified Saints Reign with Christ

In Revelation 20:4, John tells us about another vision: "And I saw thrones, and they sat upon them, and judgment was given unto them." These royal people are kingly priests who reign with Christ for a thousand years:

> And I saw the souls of them that were beheaded for the witness of Jesus and for the word of God, and which had not worshipped the beast, neither his image, neither had received his mark upon their foreheads, or in their hands; and they lived and reigned with Christ a thousand years (Revelation 20:4).

The thousand years refers to the same period in which the Devil is bound with respect to Gog and Magog. In that entire period, these martyrs reign with Christ. They are the glorified saints.

John speaks of a first resurrection: "But the rest of the dead lived not again until the thousand years were finished. This is the first resurrection" (Revelation 20:5).

Pre-millennialists believe the "first resurrection" refers to the bodily resurrection of believers at the end of the age when Christ returns. They believe the saints are given new bodies at this time. However, the "this" in verse 5 refers back to the souls mentioned in verse 4. So when John says, "This is the first resurrection," the "this" in verse 5 refers back to what is going on with the "souls" mentioned in verse 4.

With respect to the "first resurrection," we are bound to the text. We are forced to say: The regeneration and the exaltation of the souls, of the martyred saints, is the "first resurrection."

Scripture speaks of the resurrection of the dead in more than one sense. In John 5:25, Jesus' words refer to regeneration: "Verily, verily, I say unto you, The hour is coming, and now is, when the dead shall hear the voice of the Son of God: and they that hear shall live." In Revelation 20:5, the "first resurrection" refers to the exaltation of the saints in glory.

John is teaching a millennial reign of martyrs in Heaven with Jesus Christ. Throughout the Book of Revelation, thrones are always in heaven, not on the earth. Therefore, this scene is heavenly, not earthly.

The parallel passage in Revelation 6:9 is significant. There, John sees under the altar the souls of the martyrs: "And when he had opened the fifth seal, I saw under the altar the souls of them that were slain for the word of God, and for the testimony which they held" (Revelation 6:9). Wherever John mentions martyrdom for the sake of Jesus, the context indicates that this includes all believers who have been obedient to their Lord.

John identifies the disembodied spirits as those who were put to death for refusing to worship the Beast. They are martyrs. When they die, John tells us that they immediately come to life and reign with Christ for a thousand years!

This is scarcely a description of a future earthly millennium characterized by universal peace; rather, it is a time characterized by persecution and suffering. People are dying because they confess Jesus Christ. They come to life and reign with Christ in Heaven until His return at the end of the age.

Revelation 20:1-6 is not a description of a future millennial reign of Christ upon the earth. It is a description of the present reign of the saints with Christ in Heaven. The reign of Christ described in these verses is a present reality. This is, therefore, a text that should bring us great comfort.

When we die, either at the hand of the Beast or because of the wages of sin, we immediately enter the presence of Christ and reign for a thousand years as priests, safe from Satan and delivered from our sins. With this glorious scene before us, let us not fear death. Instead, let us confess Jesus as Lord with great courage.

When the Thousand Years are Expired

Revelation 20:7-9a explains what happens next. After a millennium, the thousand years, the sound of a key is once again heard turning the lock and the Devil is freed. Through the agency of the beast, the final Antichrist, Satan will deceive the nations for the express purpose of waging war upon the church. The Devil is released from his restrictions. It is like the time before the Flood.

God will allow the Devil to deceive the nations once more. He will muster his forces to disperse falsehood worldwide. He will do this through the Antichrist and the false prophet.

In Revelation 20:7-8, John mentions the mysterious God and Magog:

> And when the thousand years are expired, Satan shall be loosed out of his prison, And shall go out to deceive the nations which are in the four quarters of the earth, Gog and Magog, to gather them together to battle: the number of whom is as the sand of the sea (Revelation 20:7-8).

Gog and Magog are two leaders of Gentile nations who attacked the Israelites, as prophesied in Ezekiel 39. Gog and Magog are pictured as a vast horde of pagans who descend upon Israel from the north. Ezekiel predicted that a vast army would invade Israel. It would be an innumerable multitude, as the sand on the seashore.

Gog is the personal name of the prince of Meshech and Tubal in Asia Minor (Ezekiel 39:1) and the "Ma" in Magog may mean "land of Gog." The names do not refer to particular nations, for neither Gog nor Magog can be identified. Rather, they are symbolic terms that refer to huge forces that come from the four corners of the earth.

The battleground is the camp of the saints and the beloved city: "And they went up on the breadth of the earth, and compassed the camp of the saints, and the beloved city" (Revelation 20:9). "The camp of the saints" emphasizes that the people of God are a pilgrim people. A camp connotes a temporary abode. Christians are a tent-dwelling people.

God sends down fire from heaven to devour His enemies: "and fire came down from God out of heaven, and devoured them" (Revelation 20:9b). In Revelation 19, we are told that the Antichrist and the false prophet are cast into the lake of brimstone. Now, Satan himself is cast into the lake of fire:

> And the devil that deceived them was cast into the lake of fire and brimstone, where the beast and the false prophet are, and shall be tormented day and night for ever and ever (Revelation 20:10).

This unholy trinity of Antichrist, false prophet, and Satan are all defeated and destroyed. They will be tormented day and night forever and ever.

The last verses of the chapter give comfort to the saints when the books are opened. God vindicates the saints and judges the wicked. All those whose names are not recorded in the book of life suffer the same destiny as Satan. The torment that the wicked must suffer is one of spiritual and mental agony. They appear before the throne of God for final judgment and then enter into the second death, which means they are forever separated from the living God.

Revelation 7:1-8

1. And after these things I saw four angels standing on the four corners of the earth, holding the four winds of the earth, that the wind should not blow on the earth, nor on the sea, nor on any tree.

2. And I saw another angel ascending from the east, having the seal of the living God: and he cried with a loud voice to the four angels, to whom it was given to hurt the earth and the sea,

3. Saying, Hurt not the earth, neither the sea, nor the trees, till we have sealed the servants of our God in their foreheads.

4. And I heard the number of them which were sealed: and there were sealed an hundred and forty and four thousand of all the tribes of the children of Israel.

5. Of the tribe of Juda, were sealed twelve thousand. Of the tribe of Reuben were sealed twelve thousand. Of the tribe of Gad were sealed twelve thousand.

6. Of the tribe of Aser were sealed twelve thousand. Of the tribe of Nepthalim were sealed twelve thousand. Of the tribe of Manasses were sealed twelve thousand.

7. Of the tribe of Simeon were sealed twelve thousand. Of the tribe of Levi were sealed twelve thousand. Of the tribe of Issachar were sealed twelve thousand.

8. Of the tribe of Zabulon were sealed twelve thousand. Of the tribe of Joseph were sealed twelve thousand. Of the tribe of Benjamin were sealed twelve thousand.

CHAPTER 6

The 144,000

Revelation 7 forms an intermission between the breaking of the sixth and seventh seals. In this intermission, a decisive answer is given to the question raised by men terrified of the wrath of the Lamb, as seen by John at the end of Revelation 6. Before the opening of the seventh seal, which will lead to the trumpet judgments, God decided to give His people an encouraging message. The wicked asked: "Who shall be able to stand?" (Revelation 6:17) This question is now answered.

John saw "four angels standing on the four corners of the earth, holding the four winds of the earth, that the wind should not blow on the earth, nor on the sea, nor on any tree" (Revelation 7:1). These angels have the remarkable job of controlling the winds.

The winds represent all the violent powers that will sweep over the earth – as depicted in the earlier seals. The aftermath of hurricanes and tornadoes should leave us in no doubt about the aptness of wind as a symbol of judgment.

Another angel flies towards John, carrying the seal of the living God. He calls out to the four angels this message: "Hurt not the earth, neither the sea, nor the trees, till we have sealed the servants of our God in their foreheads" (Revelation 7:3).

Ridiculous Speculations

Jehovah's Witnesses and pre-millennial dispensationalists have produced ridiculous speculations about the identity of these 144,000.

The Jehovah's Witnesses proudly identify the 144,000 as themselves! They applied this vision to themselves even though they were neither Jews nor Christians. They ran into difficulty, however, when their group grew beyond 144,000.

After this, they started another category of 144,000, now believing there was an earthly band of 144,000 and a heavenly band of 144,000. If you believed their doctrines in the early part of the 20th Century, you could belong to the heavenly band. When this cult grew to more than 288,000 members, they created a third band called "the servant band."

If you become a Jehovah's Witness today, you must come in at the servant level. This is one example of how this passage has been hijacked for sectarian purposes.

This vision has also been misinterpreted by dispensational pre-millennialists. Ray Stedman claimed that the 144,000 are a special group of Jews whom we could call "Christ's commandos." They supposedly are ethnic Jews, who will exist after the rapture.

They are literally 12,000 men from each tribe of ethnic Israel who will be a great company of preachers. So the 144,000 are a unique group of Jews selected to proclaim the gospel after the rapture.

Stedman argued that the term "Israel" must be interpreted in accordance with its normal Old and New Testament usage as a reference to the physical descendants of Abraham, Isaac, and Jacob. It is true that the tribal records were lost when the Romans sacked Jerusalem in A.D. 70. But Stedman argues that God knows who belongs to each tribe.

Pre-millennialists also teach that the so-called "ten lost tribes" were never lost. God is not done with the nation of Israel; in the future, the Jewish people will become the greatest missionary force the world has seen. The result of their mission work will be a redeemed Israel and many saved Gentiles.

In line with Stedman's interpretation, arguments are given for why the 144,000 cannot symbolize the church. Robert Thomas writes, "No clear-cut example of the church being called 'Israel' exists in the New Testament or in ancient church writings until A.D. 160...This fact is crippling to any attempt to identify Israel as the church in Rev. 7:4."

It is claimed that the Bible predicted that ethnic Jews would one day preach the "gospel of the kingdom" throughout all the cities of Israel. This gospel is the message of the earthly, millennial kingdom. Jesus supposedly predicts this: "But when they persecute you in this city, flee ye into another: for verily I say unto you, Ye shall not have gone over the cities of Israel, till the Son of man become" (Matthew 10:23).

Ray Stedman argues, "Our Lord seems to leap over the whole of the present age to the day when a group of Jews (not twelve but twelve squared, times the cube of ten—144,000), will be sent out into all the world." These 144,000 will survive the wrath of God and enter into a millennial kingdom on earth.

Who Are the 144,000?

We believe that John sees the new Israel – the Israel of God. The 144,000 represent Christ's Church on earth at any one time. Looking at Scripture, we find a number of reasons to support this.

First, the Apostle Paul repeatedly refers to the church as the true Israel. Consider four passages. Paul teaches in Romans 2:29, "But he is a Jew, which is one inwardly; and circumcision is that of the heart." You, who have heart circumcision, are Jews – you are the Israel of God.

In Romans 9, Paul states that true Israel, in the old as well as the new dispensation, was spiritual, not carnal, Israel: "For they are not all Israel, which are of Israel" (Romans 9:6). You, who have the faith of Abraham, are true spiritual Israel.

Paul teaches there is no difference between ethnic Jews and ethnic Gentiles in the New Testament: "For there is no difference between the Jew and the Greek: for the same Lord over all is rich unto all that call upon him" (Romans 10:12).

Finally, in Galatians 6:16, Paul teaches: "And as many as walk according to this rule, peace be on them, and mercy, and upon the Israel of God." So we see this vision is not of Israel as a nation, but the true Israel, the spiritual Israel, the church, described by the Apostle Paul as "the Israel of God."

Second, the Apostle Peter calls the New Testament church "a chosen generation, a royal priesthood, a holy nation, a peculiar people" (I Peter 2:9).

Peter takes descriptions that were given to Old Testament Israel and applies them to the New Testament church. The church is the new Israel. As a New Testament believer, you are the Israel of God! The Jewish Christ has made elect Gentiles citizens of His Kingdom.

God's Election

That there were 12,000 sealed from each tribe speaks of God's elect purpose. Mere random human choosing would not end up with such a perfect number.

The number is symbolic. As mentioned earlier, in Scripture, ten is a number of completion. None can be added to this number. Notice that only 12,000 of each tribe are taken. It is emphasized in the Greek where 13 times we have the phrase "out of" where the English has "of." This reminds us that only a portion of the whole is saved.

They are not all Israel who are of Israel. This is the elect remnant among the confessing members of the church on earth. They are the elect of God – they are numbered and listed.

Twelve is the number of God's covenant people in this world; there were twelve sons of Jacob, twelve tribes, and twelve apostles. Therefore, this number is symbolic of the complete number of the predestinated who are living on earth at any one time in the last days.

These Jewish and Gentile Christians are called the "servants of God." In other words, the 144,000 are symbolic of the church militant. The church militant is composed of all of the true Christians who exist at one point in human history.

A Military Census

What we have in Revelation 7 is similar to the military censuses we find in the Old Testament. In verses 5 through 8, we have a list of the 12 tribes and how many of each tribe are sealed. A number of things stand out in this list. Although Reuben was the firstborn, Judah is listed first. Reuben forfeited his birthright because of his sexual sin with his father's concubine.

Second, the omission of Dan in favor of Levi is also unusual. Dan was probably omitted because of the tribe's penchant for idolatry. One of the golden calves was set up in Dan. Jacob predicted: "Dan shall be a serpent by the way, an adder in the path, that biteth the horse heels, so that his rider shall fall backward" (Genesis 49:17). This is a poetic portrayal of the treachery of Dan in introducing apostasy by taking Micah's false priest and ephod (Judges 18).

Third, Ephraim is also omitted and Joseph, his father, is mentioned. This is probably because Ephraim led in the defection from the line of David. Jeroboam the son of Nebat, who caused Israel to sin, was from the tribe of Ephraim (I Kings 11:26).

Revelation 7 appears to contain a census of the church militant. In Numbers 1, we find a Biblical background for this type of numbering and listing. There God commanded Moses:

> Take ye the sum of all the congregation of the children of Israel, after their families, by the house of their fathers, with the number of their names, every male by their polls; From twenty years old and upward, all that are able to go forth to war in Israel: thou and Aaron shall number them by their armies (Numbers 1:2-3).

The census of Numbers 1 is a military census. It records "all that are able to go forth to war in Israel" (Numbers 1:3). This idea is also repeated in Numbers 1:45.

The numbering of the elect in Revelation 7 is a military census. Revelation 7 pictures the church as an army. Do not let this vision mislead you.

This is not some tribulation force made up of converts of those who were left behind. It is an army of Christian believers. They march forth with the Word and sacraments. We see a church that possesses apparent weaknesses, and yet her weaknesses are her strength. By her humility, suffering, and spiritual weapons, she battles. They will fight with their radical love ethic.

As believers, we are numbered among the church militant. We are a church under attack by Satan. As a roll is kept in Heaven, so there is a roll on earth. Church membership is important. Because of the attacks of the Devil, it is necessary for God's people to gather together as the body of Christ. It is vital for us to fellowship in the Spirit with believers and to feed regularly on God's Word and to be nourished with the visible Word in the sacraments. A soldier cannot fight the battle alone.

The Sealing

John saw an angel arrive with the seal of the Living God (Revelation 7:2). A seal is a signet ring which kings would use to stamp the wax on a document to prove the authenticity of a royal decree. A seal denoted ownership and protection. When the pope excommunicated Luther, he dripped wax onto the document and then impressed his papal seal upon it. A seal was used to safeguard the contents of a letter from those who were not supposed to read it, to prove that a bull of excommunication had come from a person with the right to give it.

In contrast to the seals of men, this seal is that of the Living God. The angel has the job of sealing the 144,000. In Ezekiel 9:3-6, we find a similar illustration – the Lord tells a man clothed in linen to put a mark on the foreheads of men *who sighed and groaned at the sin in Jerusalem.* Those who did not receive the mark on their foreheads would be slain in the coming destruction of Jerusalem.

The Seal

We do not have to guess what this seal is. This seal is the person of the Holy Spirit. Paul told the Ephesians: "And grieve not the holy Spirit of God, whereby ye are sealed unto the day of redemption" (Eph. 4:30).

He wrote: "Now he which stablisheth us with you in Christ, and hath anointed us, is God; Who hath also sealed us, and given the earnest of the Spirit in our hearts" (II Corinthians 1:21-22).

We bear the stamp of the Holy Spirit. He is the mark of God's ownership of us. Our ownership can never be changed again. This seal cannot be obliterated. The Holy Spirit will never abandon us. We have the imprint of the Holy Spirit – His presence in our life. As we have the sealing of the Holy Spirit, we are assured that we are numbered and listed in the census of the church militant.

The 144,000 are Spirit-filled Christians. The seal is placed on the foreheads of the saints and will allow them to be readily identified.

Beware of how the Antichrist will ape God by sealing his followers (Revelation 13:16-17). Do not receive the mark of the Beast.

Our Security

If you are a believer, the seal of God is upon you. Judgment will come, but you have nothing to fear. The woes of the book of Revelation are written against the wicked. God punished the sins of His people in Christ, their Substitute, to the full satisfaction of His justice. Since the Holy Spirit seals, you are safeguarded against attack.

In what sense are we immune to the horrific judgments still to be poured out – the trumpet judgments and bowl judgments? How are we to understand the security of the people of God? Does this mean that plagues will not touch the 144,000?

Our sealing does not mean God will protect us from the murderous efforts of the Antichrist and his henchmen. Believers will also suffer the consequences of the judgments that God pours out upon the wicked.

The idea is not that God will preserve the physical lives of believers, but He will preserve them. The physical deaths of believers will not be a result of God's wrath, but the means by which God ushers them into His presence. Spiritually, we cannot be touched or hurt by the plagues and persecutions.

Revelation 13:1-7

1. And I stood upon the sand of the sea, and saw a beast rise up out of the sea, having seven heads and ten horns, and upon his horns ten crowns, and upon his heads the name of blasphemy.

2. And the beast which I saw was like unto a leopard, and his feet were as the feet of a bear, and his mouth as the mouth of a lion: and the dragon gave him his power, and his seat, and great authority.

3. And I saw one of his heads as it were wounded to death; and his deadly wound was healed: and all the world wondered after the beast.

4. And they worshipped the dragon which gave power unto the beast: and they worshipped the beast, saying, Who is like unto the beast? Who is able to make war with him?

5. And there was given unto him a mouth speaking great things and blasphemies; and power was given unto him to continue forty and two months.

6. And he opened his mouth in blasphemy against God, to blaspheme his name, and his tabernacle, and them that dwell in heaven.

7. And it was given unto him to make war with the saints, and to overcome them: and power was given him over all kindreds, and tongues, and nations.

Revelation 13:11-13

11. And I beheld another beast coming up out of the earth; and he had two horns like a lamb, and he spake as a dragon.

12. And he exerciseth all the power of the first beast before him, and causeth the earth and them which dwell therein to worship the first beast, whose deadly wound was healed.

13. And he doeth great wonders, so that he maketh fire come down from heaven on the earth in the sight of men,

CHAPTER 7

The Beastly Minions
of the Dragon

John sees the great red dragon standing upon the lakeshore as two beasts rise from the sea and the earth. The dragon has gone to the seashore to summon help. He gathers two minions, two servile followers. The two beasts of Revelation 13 are the helpers of the dragon. These are two agents whom the dragon uses to attack the church.

The first beast is a monster of indescribable horror. The second has a harmless appearance and for that reason, is even more dangerous than the first. But neither operates on its own authority; they are slaves of the Devil.

The First Beast Out of the Sea

In the vision, John sees a beast gradually emerge out of the sea. First, he only sees ten horns that are covered with seven crowns. Next, seven lion heads appear with names of blasphemy. Then comes the body – like a leopard, large and fierce. Finally, he sees the feet of a bear. The last thing he mentions is that the beast has the "the mouth of a lion." Growling, roaring, and intimidating; it is anxious to destroy.

This kind of beast could give a child nightmares. The beast, rising out of the sea, is not a creature like man, made in the divine image, but is a deformed wild animal, under the control of Satan. The sea represents the surging of the nations and their governments. The sea, in its unrest, is a picture of the troubled, sinful world.

The Second Beast

John sees a second animal – a lamb that comes out of the earth. It looks like an innocent lamb, but it is a beast, clearly trying to ape Christ. This lamb does not look like it was slain and has only two horns. What betrays this innocent-looking animal is that when it speaks, it has the deep, powerful, awful voice of a dragon.

This second beast is a servant of the first. It exercises the authority of the first beast. It performs many tricks and pseudo- miracles to deceive men.

Together, these two represent the final Antichrist. The political aspect of the Antichrist is pictured in the first beast and the religious or spiritual aspect in the second beast.

What is interesting about the first beast is that it is a composite of three animals; it has the head of a lion, the paws of a bear, and the legs and tail of a leopard. In the book of Daniel, we find four similar beasts representing four successive world empires. In Daniel 7, we find that each one of those beasts is a picture of a typical antichristian kingdom: Babylon, Media- Persia, Greece, and finally Rome. Here, this composite beast cannot symbolize merely one empire or government; it must indicate all antichristian governments and especially the final worldwide kingdom.

The ten horns and the ten crowns clearly are symbolic of political dominion. In ancient times, the horns of strong animals were used as pictures of military force. Crowns pictured kingly rule. The dragon has the same number of heads and the same number of crowns. This beast wears the crowns on its horns, rather than on its heads. In other words, it is the dragon that rules, but the beast executes its plans.

The seven heads symbolize seven antichristian empires that succeed one another in history. The fact that one head received a death stroke, which had been healed, receives that one of these seven empires ceased to persecute, but afterward resumed its former role. He thinks the head is Rome, first under Nero, and then later under Domitian. Herman Hoeksema thinks the wound was the Tower of Babel. Others think it was the cross.

The sea beast symbolizes the antichristian kingdoms by which Satan fights against the church. First it was Egypt, Assyria, Babylon, Persia, Greece, then Rome – all worldly governments directed against the church.

Hendriksen says that the first beast is Satan's hand representing the persecuting power of Satan operating in and through the nations and governments of this world. The lamb- like dragon out of the earth symbolizes Satan's mind representing false religions and philosophies of the world. It pictures the spiritual aspect of the Antichristian kingdom.

The second beast is later called the false prophet in Revelation 19:20 and symbolizes false religion and false philosophy in whatever forms it takes in the end times. Although this beast outwardly resembles a lamb, it inwardly conceals the dragon. In other words, the beast looks like a nice little lamb, but its speech reveals its inner character.

Notice that this beast does not just promote pagan philosophy, but heresy, teachings that it spins off as Christian doctrine. False philosophies and religions will undergird the one- world government. Today, we already see

Islam undergirds the government of Iran; atheistic-communism undergirds the government of China. These two beasts work in cooperation.

Antichrist: A Single Man who is The Man of Sin

The attractive and inspiring Antichrist will have a worldwide kingdom. He will preside over a time of unprecedented peace and wealth. The whole earth will wonder after the beast. All nations will freely and willingly obey the one government. Schools, universities, and churches will be under its jurisdiction, as well as commerce and industry.

Herman Hoeksema writes about the possibility that there will be no single man who is the Antichrist. He emphasizes that a group of men could be the final Antichrist: "It makes no difference now whether this governing head is a person or a group of persons, a sort of central committee, which rules the whole world."

However, we find good reason to believe that one man will be the final Antichrist. Paul speaks of the "man of sin" (II Thessalonians 2:3).

Already now, we see signs of antichrists in popes. They might seem fragile and innocent like a lamb, but if you listen to their teachings about justification, the church, the sacraments, or indulgences, you hear the voice of the dragon. Likewise, the mainline Presbyterian, Methodist, and Episcopal Church are filled with ministers who are mouthpieces of the second beast.

In an attempt to mimic how the church worships Christ, the Antichrist, this false prophet, inspires and demands that men worship the first beast. As the reprobate worship the beast, they give Satan what he wants most in the entire world: worship. At the end, men – through the Devil's deceptions – will seem very spiritual and religious.

To that end, the false prophet does great wonders. By his miracles he deceives people to make an image to worship the beast. Since the Antichrist cannot be everywhere, statues are set up around the world. If these images are literal, they could be placed in churches so that the Antichrist fulfills Paul's description of the Antichrist:

Who opposeth and exalteth himself above all that is called God, or that is worshipped; so that he as God sitteth in the temple of God, showing himself that he is God (II Thessalonians 2:4).

The Antichrist will persecute and kill Christians in the great tribulation. He will be in a position to do this because of his one- world government. He makes war with the saints.

The Mark of the Beast

Notice that the believer receives a seal, but the unbeliever a mere mark. The lamb-like dragon also wants to mark out and identify those who belong to him. John tells us: "If any man worships the beast" he will "receive the mark on his forehead" (Revelation 14:9). Again in Revelation 14:11, we are told that those who "worship the beast" will "receive the mark of his name." Those who worship the beast will receive something that identifies them as an adherent of the Antichrist.

Early Christians were forced to produce a slip of paper that proved that they had offered a sacrifice of incense to the emperor as Lord. When they would not produce this sign of adherence to Caesar as Lord, they were thrown to the lions.

It is not clear that the mark of the beast is a physical mark on the forehead or right hand. The forehead symbolizes the mind, the thought-life or worldview of a person. The right hand stands for one's actions. So, receiving the mark on the forehead or right hand indicates that the person believes the lies of Antichrist and obeys Antichrist.

There has been much speculation about the identity of this mark. Some have thought the Antichrist will use microchip implants.

Those who refuse to receive the mark of the beast will be boycotted. They will not be permitted to buy or sell or carry on any business. This can be taken literally and symbolically. For example, even today, if you are a Christian in the academic world, you may be passed by for promotions because you reject the spirit of Antichrist that is already at work in the world.

However, to receive the mark is to perish. For, the number of the beast spells his end. It is 666 – the number of man. Man was created on the sixth day. Six is not seven and never will be. It fails to attain to perfection. The Antichrist is given the number 666 to symbolize that rebellious mankind reaches its apex in him. But he falls short of 777. Victory is on the side of the covenant people, for our number is 7. The number six is symbolic of man's labor apart from rest. There is no rest for the wicked.

In the end times, the elect of God will not go along with Antichrist's program. They will do valiantly. Their names are written in the book of life from the foundation of the world.

12. Beloved, think it not strange concerning the fiery trial which is to try you, as though some strange thing happened unto you:

13. But rejoice, inasmuch as ye are partakers of Christ's sufferings; that, when his glory shall be revealed, ye may be glad also with exceeding joy.

14. If ye be reproached for the name of Christ, happy are ye; for the spirit of glory and of God resteth upon you: on their part he is evil spoken of, but on your part he is glorified.

15. But let none of you suffer as a murderer, or as a thief, or as an evildoer, or as a busybody in other men's matters.

16. Yet if any man suffer as a Christian, let him not be ashamed; but let him glorify God on this behalf.

17. For the time is come that judgment must begin at the house of God: and if it first begin at us, what shall the end be of them that obey not the gospel of God?

18. And if the righteous scarcely be saved, where shall the ungodly and the sinner appear?

19. Wherefore let them that suffer according to the will of God commit the keeping of their souls to him in well doing, as unto a faithful Creator.

CHAPTER 8

Facing a Fiery Future

The Need for a Solid Theology

The Bible teaches that faithful Christians will suffer fiery trials in the future. In the face of this future suffering, we need to have a solid theology that will enable us to endure. We need to have spiritual insight into the reason for persecution in order that we might rejoice and in the midst of it, give glory to our faithful Savior.

Persecution is not something that should be seen as alien to the Christian life. From the very beginning, believers have been attacked. Cain killed Abel because his own works were evil and his brother's works were righteous. The Master, who Christians follow, was persecuted and murdered.

The Bible teaches that suffering is not meaningless, but purposeful, involving testing and refining. Christians are strangers and pilgrims in an alien world where Satan is the god and prince (II Corinthians 4:3-4).

Jesus predicted fiery trials: "But beware of men: for they will deliver you up to the councils, and they will scourge you in their synagogues" (Matthew 10:17).

Jesus warned: "Think not that I am come to send peace on earth: I came not to send peace, but a sword. For I am come to set a man at variance against his father, and the daughter against her mother, and the daughter in law against her mother in law" (Matthew 10:34-35).

Every Christian who lives a godly life experiences a certain amount of persecution. Unbelievers will find fault and criticize. Peter speaks about this kind of "normal persecution" in the first part of this letter. But I Peter 4:12 predicts a "fiery trial" that had begun to overtake the church.

This was official persecution. Up until this time, Christianity as a religion had been tolerated by the Roman Empire because it was viewed as a "sect" of Judaism, and the Romans had a long-standing agreement with the Jews that allowed them to practice their religion freely. The Romans found that the Jews were intransigent in the matter of their religion. After the Babylonian captivity, the Jews were cured of idolatry. They did not want to worship the Roman gods and goddesses. They would rather die than do so.

How do you deal with such obstinate people? The Romans realized that they needed to give the Jews a bye when it came to worship of the Roman gods.

In the early church, Roman magistrates often defended the Apostle Paul when he was brought before them. They pointed out that Paul had not violated any Roman laws by proclaiming Jesus. But things were about to change. Under Nero the imperial government began actively to persecute Christians.

In order to endure persecution, we need to know what God is like and how He is at work in our lives. If we have a false and shallow theology, we will not be prepared to face fiery persecution.

This theology says that God has saved us to make us happy. The health/wealth gospel is a shallow theology that will not enable believers to withstand persecution. If a person believes God saved him in order to take away his pain and give him good health and long life, how will he deal with imprisonment, beatings, malnourishment, and death? A true and deep theology will help us anticipate and endure persecution.

Peter wrote, "Wherefore let them that suffer according to the will of God commit the keeping of their souls to him in well doing, as unto a faithful Creator" (I Peter 4:19). We may weep due to the pain, but we will not be surprised because the work of the Holy Spirit and our knowledge of God will not let us be thrown into confusion or uncertainty.

Tried with Fiery Trials

In Scripture, the image of "fire" is often applied to testing or persecution. In the Old Testament, fire was a symbol of the holiness of God. Peter saw the image of fire as a refining process, rather than a severe judgment. The allusion is to the smelter's fire. As gold is refined, so the believer's faith is tested through suffering.

God loves to test the authenticity of our faith. He wants us to understand the value of faith and growing in faith. The Word says the trial of our faith is "of greater worth than gold."

God hates sin so much and loves us so much that He will spare us no pain to rid us of what He hates and what is bad for us.

It is comforting to know persecution does not just happen. The persecutors tempt us to renounce our faith, but God sovereignly uses persecution to purify His people. In these last days, the Scriptures tell us that fiery trials are coming.

On January 19, 1981, a group of terrorists called "M-19" kidnapped Wycliffe translator Chet Bitterman. Chet's wife Brenda and their two little children waited 48 days. On March 7, the terrorists shot Chet Bitterman through the heart and left his body on a bus in Bogota.

In November, 1998, Muslim terrorists in Pakistan murdered nine Christians in the northeastern town of Noshehra. The father of the family was a man of prayer. This offended some extremist Muslim groups because even Muslims would approach this Christian man to pray on their behalf. These Christians were butchered with sharp knives and most of them had their throats slashed, even the one-month-old grandson.

During the Cultural Revolution in China, innumerable Christians were hauled in front of crowds and publicly abused. Their arms were put in the "jet" position, behind them, and then they were jumped on and stomped to death. Countless believers were separated from their families and thrown into the work camps.

Peter warns: "But let none of you suffer as a murderer, or as a thief, or as an evildoer, or as a busybody in other men's matters" (I Peter 4:15). He speaks directly to the confessing Christian.

May no Christian dishonor the name of God by living publicly in sin as a gang-banger, petty thief, shoplifter, or any kind of evildoer. You better feel shame if you suffer as an evildoer.

Peter adds a strange word: busybody. This is the only occurrence of this word in the New Testament and in all Greek manuscripts. It has the word for a bishop or elder in it. Apparently, he is thinking about someone who usurps authority in matters that are not within his provenance. He interferes in the affairs of others and, through excess of zeal, tries to get them to conform to his personal opinions.

If you suffer because others condemn you as a busybody, be ashamed.

Judgment Begins at the House of God

One reason for persecution is that God judges and chastises the church. Peter writes: "For the time is come that judgment must begin at the house of God: and if it first begin at us, what shall the end be of them that obey not the gospel of God?" (I Peter 4:17). In the Old Testament, God would hold His people accountable first.

If God is this hard on the church, how much harder will He be on those who do not obey the gospel! When God's fiery judgments fall on the wicked world, they will be incinerated! The way of the wicked might appear smooth in this life; after all, they are not the objects of persecution. Yet the way that leads away from God has, at the end, a terrible precipice.

Peter teaches: "And if the righteous scarcely be saved, where shall the ungodly and the sinner appear?" (I Peter 4:18) The argument is from the lesser to the greater.

If God spares not His own children, whom He loves, how dreadful will be His severity against His enemies! The phrase "scarcely saved" means "saved with difficulty." This explains the necessity of trials. We are so easily attached to this world and so loathe to exercise faith in God that God considers it necessary to chastise us.

Exulting in Persecutions!

As Christians, we should not only expect trials, but exult in them: "Yet if any man suffer as a Christian, let him not be ashamed; but let him glorify God on this behalf" (I Peter 4:16). The conditional statement, "if any man suffer as a Christian," is a first-class condition. Peter implies that the "if" statement is true. In other words, he is saying, "If any man suffers as a Christian - and you will - then be unashamed."

About fifteen years before Peter wrote his first letter, the name "Christian" was first used in Antioch. It was a term of reproach. Tacitus writes about what happened after Rome burned and Nero fiddled: "Nero substituted as culprits, and punished with the utmost refinements of cruelty, a class of men...whom the crowd styled Christians."

The mark of a Christian is that he experiences deeper and greater joy in being dishonored with Christ than he does in being honored by men. Christians should exult in trials. This is no blithe joy. Peter was realistic about how vicious the enemies of God's people could be.

No one should read Peter and suppose he imagined Sudanese Christians could blithely surrender their children to Islamic militia to undergo forced conversions and be sold into slavery - with a smile on their faces. He is not saying parents should be gleeful when their daughters are kidnapped and enslaved for their Christian confession.

Peter's thinking is much deeper, much more profound than that. He is not speaking of "joy" as a flippant happiness.

He is speaking of a deep emotional state that finds strength and comfort in the toughest of times. The persecuted Christian has a profound awareness that it is worth it to suffer for Jesus. He has a deep awareness that God is on the throne. Christians have this "inexpressible joy," and it transforms our outlook on life. Our life is founded on the reality that God loves us.

Peter commands persecuted Christians: "But rejoice, inasmuch as ye are partakers of Christ's sufferings; that, when his glory shall be revealed, ye may be glad also with exceeding joy" (I Peter 4:13).

Keep on rejoicing because your sufferings as a Christian are evidence of your union with Christ. The church does not share in Jesus' redemptive sufferings – they were vicarious, but God has ordained that the church as the body of Christ, should also suffer a certain amount.

Mature people know that life includes some "postponed pleasures." We pay a price today in order to have enjoyments in the future. The piano student may not enjoy practicing, but he looks forward to the pleasure of playing beautiful music one day. If we suffer now, we can be certain of glory later. Christians will be overjoyed when Christ returns in glory!

It is far better to suffer a little for Christ now than be damned by Christ forever: "And he that taketh not his cross, and followeth after me, is not worthy of me. He that findeth his life shall lose it: and he that loseth his life for my sake shall find it" (Matthew 10:38-39).

God might appear to be severe toward the church, allowing the wicked to pass their lives in continued pleasures. John Calvin wrote:

> God so regulates his judgments in this world, that he fattens the wicked for the day of slaughter. He therefore passes by their many sins, and, as it were, connives at them. In the meantime, he restores by corrections his own children, for whom he has a care, to the right way, whenever they depart from it.

Joseph Tson, a Romanian pastor who stood up to Ceausescu's repressions of Christianity, wrote:

> This union with Christ...means that I am not a lone fighter here: I am an extension of Jesus Christ. When I was beaten in Romania, He suffered in my body. It is

not my suffering: I only had the honor to share His sufferings.

When we suffer as Christians, we should consider it an honor to be lumped together with Christ. Jesus said:

> The disciple is not above his master, nor the servant above his lord. It is enough for the disciple that he be as his master, and the servant as his lord. If they have called the master of the house Beelzebub, how much more shall they call them of his household? (Matthew 10:24- 25).

Christ is With Us in the Fiery Furnace

When the three friends of Daniel were cast into the fiery furnace, they discovered that they were not alone (Daniel 3:23-25). As Christians, we can face fiery trials knowing that the Spirit of glory and of God will uphold us: "If ye be reproached for the name of Christ, happy are ye; for the spirit of glory and of God resteth upon you: on their part he is evil spoken of, but on your part he is glorified" (I Peter 4:14).

It is beautiful how the Holy Spirit is called "The Spirit of glory" and "the Spirit of God." He is the Spirit of glory because He is glorious.

We get the strength to face persecution from the Spirit of glory and of God. "But when they deliver you up, take no thought how or what ye shall speak: for it shall be given you in that same hour what ye shall speak. For it is not ye that speak, but the Spirit of your Father which speaketh in you" (Matthew 10:19, 20). The Spirit carries out a special ministry to those who suffer for the name of Jesus Christ.

The Apostle Paul wrote how, at his Roman trial, no one stood by him. The Holy Spirit will stand by us when there is no one else. He will sustain our faith. As Stephen was being stoned to death, the Holy Spirit gave the deacon a glimpse of Jesus Christ on the Father's right hand. The Spirit, too, will give us glimpses of glory. He will cause us to magnify Christ in our death. The Holy Spirit will help us die!

As Christians, it is possible to face fiery trials and death because we can entrust our souls to a faithful Creator. Entrusting our soul is to deposit it for safekeeping with God. This is a constant work, but we can do it because God is our Creator. His faithfulness will not fail.

We commit our souls to God by means of well-doing: "Commit the keeping of their souls to him in well doing, as unto a faithful Creator" (I Peter 4:19). As a Christian, do not seek vengeance for those who hurt you personally. Rather, pray for them and seek to lead them to Jesus.

The Christian soldier fights by his love. The martyr Stephen is our example. With his last breath he prayed for his persecutors: "Lord, lay not this sin to their charge" (Acts 7:60).

Revelation 17:1-6

1. And there came one of the seven angels which had the seven vials, and talked with me, saying unto me, Come hither; I will shew unto thee the judgment of the great whore that sitteth upon many waters:

2. With whom the kings of the earth have committed fornication, and the inhabitants of the earth have been made drunk with the wine of her fornication.

3. So he carried me away in the spirit into the wilderness: and I saw a woman sit upon a scarlet colored beast, full of names of blasphemy, having seven heads and ten horns.

4. And the woman was arrayed in purple and scarlet colour, and decked with gold and precious stones and pearls, having a golden cup in her hand full of abominations and filthiness of her fornication:

5. And upon her forehead was a name written, MYSTERY, BABYLON THE GREAT, THE MOTHER OF HARLOTS AND ABOMINATIONS OF THE EARTH.

6. And I saw the woman drunken with the blood of the saints, and with the blood of the martyrs of Jesus: and when I saw her, I wondered with great admiration."

CHAPTER 9

The Great Whore: the Antichrist's Mistress

In the vision recorded in Revelation 17, John was amazed at the sight of a great whore. We are going to explore who she is and why she is called "Babylon the Great."

I worry that American Christians have too naïve a view of the sinful world. Reformed Christians believe they are to glorify God in business, education, politics, and every sphere of life. They also affirm that the world, God made, is good. We also derive many cultural benefits from a world that, as a whole, is in rebellion against God, of which Satan is said to be the prince.

The vision of a great whore reminds us that the sinful world and the false church are seductive and dangerous. This description of the great whore is a warning to us about how we are to live antithetically. There is a conflict between the church and the great whore, and the calling of believers is to live against the sinful world. Have you heard the call to come out of Babylon?

John sees a strange scene: a prostitute riding a scarlet beast. She is dressed like a prostitute with expensive and gaudy garments and jewelry. She is in the wilderness and sits upon many waters, perhaps above an oasis.

She has been drinking and is drunk. Like a famous Roman prostitute, she publishes her name. We can picture the name as written on a band on her forehead: "Mystery, Babylon the Great, the Mother of Harlots and abominations of the earth." This whore is a picture of the false church that commits spiritual fornication.

Wrong Explanations

Some would say she pictures the city of Rome, as the seat of the persecuting Roman Empire. A lot of hay has been made out of the fact that the seven heads of the beast are interpreted in verse 9 as being seven mountains "on which the woman sitteth."

The problem is that there were no mountains in Rome, only hills. Also notice that the whore is not identified with the seven mountains, she merely sits on them. The seven mountains are further explained to be seven kings or kingdoms. Like a mountain juts up, these kingdoms jut up over others. Therefore, the mountains picture the seven world powers of Antichrist.

Second, she has been identified as the Roman Catholic Church, which has its headquarters in the city of Rome. We, however, have seen that the early Roman Catholic Church was often orthodox. In addition, the apostate church is not only found in the Roman Catholic Church.

The False Church

The correct understanding of the identity of the great whore is probably what Herman Hoeksema argued; she is a picture of the false church. In Scripture, a harlot is generally a woman who has been married, but has shamefully forsaken her husband for other men – strangers.

Spiritually, fornication, in Scripture, indicates the breaking of the covenant. In Ezekiel 16:8-22, the Scriptures give a complete picture of the spiritual harlot. Outward members of the Old Testament covenant received the outward benefits of the covenant, but employed them in the service of strange gods. They departed from their rightful husband. Elsewhere in the Bible, we find cities called harlots: Jerusalem (Isaiah 1:21-23) and Ninevah (Jonah 3:4).

The whore is symbolic of spiritual apostasy. A prostitute seduces men to sleep with her in return for payment. She dresses seductively to lure married men to her bed. In the same way, Babylon seduces people away from God and makes them unfaithful. Likewise, the prostitute of Revelation pictures the false church and the attractiveness of heresy and immorality.

Yet there is more to this whore than being the false church. For, she is also a city called Babylon. This might seem strange, but this apes the church because the church is sometimes called the bride of Christ, and yet elsewhere is pictured as the New Jerusalem descending out of Heaven. So we see the church as a holy bride and a city.

The connection between a whore and the city of Babylon comes out in her name: "Mystery, Babylon the Great, the Mother of Harlots and abominations of the earth." It is clear in Revelation 18 that Babylon pictures the city of man or the city of this world. She pictures human civilization as it develops in antithesis to God, according to the spirit of Antichrist.

As a whore, she is represents how false Christianity attempts to mimic the church. She is a picture of the deceptive nature of heresy. She is the mother of apostasy and cults and heresy. The false church continues to preach and administer the sacraments and claims to worship God, but she is actually the mistress of the Antichrist.

As a city, she is a picture of the organic life of apostate mankind as he develops civilization. It is the same in the church. We distinguish between the institutional life of the church and her life as organism.

Christ is head in the institutional life of the church as the saints gather to hear the Word preached by a teaching elder and where Christ rules through the ruling elders and shows mercy officially through the deacons. But Christ also rules in the daily lives of believers as they serve Him in whatever their vocation is. The latter is the organic life of the church of God.

So it is with the false church. She has her institutional existence, but she also has an organic life, in which men and women in their vocations serve the Antichrist.

The figure of the woman changes into that of a great city controlling the affairs of the world and is a center of all the movements of philosophy, religion, science, art, literature, commerce, and industry in the world.

In the city of this world, the children of the Devil develop civilization in line with the teaching of the false church. This civilization involves all of the seductions and pleasures of sin. This earthly city, Babylon, is to be seen in contrast to the heavenly city – the New Jerusalem.

Babylon pictures apostate mankind and his cultural products used to entice and seduce the believer away from God (Revelation 18:11).

The whore seduces men to worship an idol. She seduces men into breaking God's commandments. Her theology is man- centered. She embodies the three methods Satan uses to attack the church. The first is brutal persecution by political power. The second is seduction by heresy. The third is to enslave men to the pleasures of sin.

Already now, the whore seduces. It is true that the great whore is a picture of the final development of the false church at the end of time. But we live in a time of great apostasy. The spirit of Antichrist is at work. The teachings of cults are attractive to sinful men because they teach that works can save them. This is a doctrine the flesh has always loved.

Who Is Seduced?

Who does the whore seduce? What is she riding? John says, "And I saw a woman sit upon a scarlet colored beast, full of names of blasphemy, having seven heads and ten horns" (Revelation 17:3). At first glance, this scarlet-covered beast seems to be the great red dragon. Upon further study, this beast refers to the first beast of Revelation 13:1 that pictures the political aspect of the Antichrist.

So, we see a very close connection between the seven heads and the ten horns and the Antichrist. The seven heads picture seven kingdoms of Antichrist throughout history. That is why John can write "And here are seven kings: five are fallen, and one is, and the other is not yet come" (Revelation 17:10). They are: Egypt, Assyria, Babylonia, Medo-Persia, Greece, Rome, and the final antichristian kingdom. The Antichrist is the final development of the antichristian kingdom.

The power of Antichrist carries her along, but she also controls the Antichrist with her fascinating fornications. The Antichrist finds that the false church helps him set up his kingdom. The city of Babylon seduces men with the hedonistic pursuit of money, wealth, and pleasures apart from God.

Babylon is a picture of the seat of the dragon. It is the city of this world from the perspective of the attractions and pleasures of sin whether they are cultured sins or sins committed in the art galleries – all are the sins of pride and self- centeredness.

The kings of the earth sleep with this harlot. This represents how the political powers of the world will find great delight in the pleasures of sin. They will use their power to cause the whore to prosper. They will use their power to obtain riches and power and satisfy the lusts of the flesh and the pride of eyes.

The great whore seduces the businessman who loves money to cheat and lie to get more. She seduces the confessing Christian in academia to keep quiet about his faith in order to rise to the top of the academic ladder. She seduces the young person to go to a movie filled with filth and sex and evil. She tempts the young woman to worship the idol of herself that is reflected in her mirror. This whore is the mother of harlots. She is the mother of the young person who tries to tempt a man or woman to commit adultery.

The wise man describes what happens to whoremongers: "Her house is the way to hell, going down to the chambers of death" (Proverbs 7:27).

In sharp contrast to the whore, we need to live antithetically. Babylon tempts us to pursue illicit sexual gratification, power, riches, and material goods in an attempt to find something that will satisfy the soul and dull the mind so that one can forget God. However, we must remember Daniel's temptation to eat King Nebuchadnezzar's food in Babylon. He turned down the Babylon's food for vegetables and water.

The Call to Spiritual Separation

John hears another voice saying, "Come out of her, my people, that ye be not partakers of her sins, and that ye receive not of our plagues" (Revelation 18:4). Now, we see how practically important it is to identify the great whore. We must refuse her seductions. If you find yourself in the arms of this whore, repent and get out. Run away like Joseph. Flee fornication. Do whatever is necessary, whether that means gouging out your eye or cutting off your hand!

The elect people of God do come out because of the efficacious call of God. Only those who have their names written in the book of life from the foundation of the world will not be amazed and seduced by the great whore. Their names are written on the marriage certificate of the Lamb. They confess their sins and trust in Christ's blood to wash away their sins. The elect reject the harlot and identify with Christ and His church, "and they that are with him are called, and chosen, and faithful" (Revelation 17:14).

Revelation 6:1-8

1. And I saw when the Lamb opened one of the seals, and I heard, as it were the noise of thunder, one of the four beasts saying, Come and see.

2. And I saw, and behold a white horse: and he that sat on him had a bow; and a crown was given unto him: and he went forth conquering, and to conquer.

3. And when he had opened the second seal, I heard the second beasts say, Come and see.

4. And there went out another horse that was red: and power was given to him that sat thereon to take peace from the earth, and that they should kill one another: and there was given unto him a great sword.

5. And when he had opened the third seal, I heard the third beast say, Come and see. And I beheld, and lo a black horse; and he that sat on him had a pair of balances in his hand.

6. And I heard a voice in the midst of the four beasts say, A measure of wheat for a penny, and three measures of barley for a penny; and see thou hurt not the oil and the wine.

7. And when he had opened the fourth seal, I heard the voice of the fourth beasts say, Come and see.

8. And I looked, and behold a pale horse: and his name that sat on him was Death, and Hell followed with him. And power was given unto them over the fourth part of the earth, to kill with sword, and with hunger, and with death, and with the beasts of the earth.

CHAPTER 10

The Four Horsemen of the Apocalypse

Very often, the book of Revelation builds on the Old Testament. Sometimes it is a commentary on Old Testament revelation.

The colors of the four horses described in Revelation 6 remind us of the colored horses the Prophet Zechariah described in Zechariah 6:1-8. White, red, and black horses appear in both passages.

One difference is that in Revelation one of the horses is pale, while the fourth horse in Zechariah was grizzled and bay. Another difference is that Zechariah saw horses with chariots while John sees horses with riders.

The four horses are symbolic of the four directions on a compass; these horses run throughout the entire earth. In Zechariah, the horses go in various directions. The black and white went to the north. The grizzled went to the south. The number of the horses signifies the extent of the horses running; they will bring destruction across the entire earth.

The vision in Revelation is clearer and more developed than Zechariah's. In Zechariah's vision the colors of the horses did not explicitly correspond with any actions, whereas in Revelation, the horse's color corresponds with the task of the rider.

The White Horse and Rider

The identity and nature of the first horse is the most difficult to discern. In the Bible and in ancient times, the color white was not only the color of *purity*, but also the color of *victory*. If the emphasis here is on victory, then this horse is symbolic of war and conquest.

God describes the war horse: "He saith among the trumpets, Ha, ha; and he smelleth the battle afar off, the thunder of the captains, and the shouting" (Job 39:25). Persian and Roman rulers rode white horses in triumphs. The description of the rider further clarifies the task of the white horse. He has a bow, which was a general weapon often used by Eastern armies. The bow and horse symbolize the use of conquering force.

The rider wears a crown. It is not a diadem (a kingly crown), but a laurel wreath, a sign of victory. This rider goes forth conquering and to conquer, signifying the lust for power and world dominion. He engages in offensive and destructive war. He is symbolic of the judgment of wars of conquest, such as Hitler's conquest of Czechoslovakia, the Soviets putting down the Hungarians, and China seizing Tibet.

This white horse symbolizes the triumph of the kingdom of Christ.

Some have argued that the rider is Christ. But everywhere that Jesus appears in the book of Revelation, He is clearly identified. In Revelation 19, the King of Kings, Christ, rides a white warhorse and has many diadems. Here, the presence of three other horsemen, who seem analogous, rules out the rider of the white horse as Christ.

The commentator Lenski and the Reformed pastor, Jay Kortering, argue that the white horse along with the rider symbolize the gospel of the kingdom as it goes out conquering to every nation. In Scripture, white is a symbol of purity, "though your sin be as scarlet they shall be as white as snow" (Isaiah 1:18). As the kingdom of Jesus advances, hearts are conquered.

In a Messianic Psalm, we do see Jesus' portrayed with a bow and arrow. Therefore, the running of the first horse might be fundamentally different from the others. It could point to the progress of the kingdom of Jesus as the gospel is preached to the nations. Then the white horse is symbolic of the triumph of the kingdom of Jesus in history as the church is gathered in from the nations.

Some commentators think the white horse is simply symbolic of military triumph. Then the running of the white horse would symbolize judgments on earth as God in His wrath sends victorious generals like Napoleons and Hitlers to punish wicked men through the sorrows of war.

The Running of the Red Horse

The color of the red horse is the color of warfare. The ancients named the red planet Mars after the Greek god of war. Red symbolizes blood and the incendiarism of war. The Greek word for "red" comes from the word for "fire." Think of the glow of Moscow burning after Napoleon's capture of it.

The rider of the red horse does not symbolize any one person. He fits with the horse since he is given a great sword with which to make war. The sword is clearly a symbol of killing. It is fitting that a large sword is given to this rider for he, throughout history, is sent to slaughter people throughout the earth. He is given the authority "to take peace from the earth, and that they should kill one another"

(Revelation 6:4).

God will take away man's peace. The running of the red horse takes peace from the world. A strong statement is made: peace is completely taken out of the earth. Examples today include the nuclear explosion underground in North Korea, the war in Iraq, and the war on terrorism. All are judgments of God upon a wicked world.

A Black Horse

John says: "And I beheld, and lo a black horse; and he that sat on him had a pair of balances in his hand" (Revelation 6:5). The color black is connected with famine where the complexion of people changes. We read of this phenomenon in Lamentations 4:8-9:

> Their visage is blacker than a coal; they are not known in the streets: their skin cleaveth to their bones; it is withered, it is become like a stick. They that be slain with the sword are better than they that be slain with hunger: for these pine away, stricken through for want of the fruits of the field.

In Lamentations 5:10, we read the confession: "Our skin was black like an oven because of the terrible famine."

The one riding on this horse holds a balance in his hand. Usually, wheat and barley were sold by the measure, just like it is sold today by the bushel. However, this passage predicts that in the famine, grain will be sold by weight. God warned that if His people walked contrary to Him, He would make them eat bread by weight:

> And when I have broken the staff of your bread, ten women shall bake your bread in one oven, and they shall deliver you your bread again by weight: and ye shall eat, and not be satisfied (Leviticus 26:26).

The Israelites experienced famine as a judgment of God against their sin.

John also hears the words: "and see thou hurt not the oil and the wine." The famine is not complete – for the oil and wine are still harvested, being the food and drink used daily by the ancient peoples. This might mean that while the poor suffer, the rich will be able to afford luxuries, for sometimes olive oil and wine are symbols of prosperity and happiness.

Thus the running of the black horse results in economic inequality with a small percentage possessing great wealth, but the majority of the population living in poverty. Marxism intended to do away with the running of the black horse as it tries to equalize income. This judgment is great, although not as all-encompassing as some to come. The black horse is still running.

The Pale Horse

The fourth and last horse is pale or greenish yellow. In Isaiah 29:22 and Jeremiah 30:6, this color is used to describe people who are faint and about to die. The power of death upon the body produces this affect. This horse represents death in all its horror. The rider is "Death" and "Hell" follows after him. This portrays the grim reaper claiming mankind.

A substantial number of the earth's population is killed: one-fourth. This is a significant judgment. Toward the end, an even greater percentage of the earth will be judged. The running of the pale horse is evident in death from wild beasts, as well as death from infinitesimally small creatures that we call germs. It is death in all its forms including gunshot, bombs, homicide and suicide. All are the effect of the running of this pale horse and its rider.

Judgment

The running of the four horses symbolizes judgment. The first four seals can generally be classified in the category of judgment. They are acts of Christ against a sinful and antagonistic world. They are calamities sent by Jesus to punish for evils committed. Judgments must take place for God is angry with a world that is in rebellion against Him.

This vision is powerful because it reveals the holiness of God. Because He is holy, He must punish and judge the sinful world. It is true that believers suffer as these horses run, but God's wrath is directed toward the wicked world. Even God's judgments on the ungodly serve for the benefit of the elect.

The second, third, and fourth horses are clearly indicative of the fact that Christ is always coming in judgment. Christ judges the sinful world as the world rejects the gospel message and fights against His kingdom.

Christ causes the four horses to bring about His final kingdom. Each of the horses has a rider who directs the horse according to His will. They are forces directed and limited by intelligent will with a definite goal. The Lamb is the One who directs the horses intelligently.

The first four seals represent judgments that occur during the time between Christ's first and second advents. God redeems the church through judgment: "Zion shall be redeemed with judgment, and her converts with righteousness" (Isaiah 1:27). God uses these judgments to deliver His church.

As the end comes, there is an intensification of judgment. Never were as many people slain in war or dead from pestilences as perished in the 20th Century. Christ is less and less restraining His righteous anger. The cycles of wrath will reach their climax when Christ returns in judgment. The running of these four horses is a sign of the times. Repeated famines in Africa should steer your mind to the second coming of Christ. So also, the war on terrorism is a sign of the times.

When we stand by Lake Michigan and see the spreading swells of a wake, we know that a boat has passed by. When we see effects of the running of the four horses, we know that Christ has passed by. War, famines, and violent death are signs that Christ is coming. The wake points to the certainty of Christ's return. The horse judgments are a direct result of Christ working in history to bring about His second coming.

Revelation 8:6-13

6. And the seven angels which had the seven trumpets prepared themselves to sound.

7. And the first angel sounded, and there followed hail and fire mingled with blood, and they were cast upon the earth: and the third part of trees was burnt up, and all green grass was burnt up.

8. And the second angel sounded, and as it were a great mountain burning with fire was cast into the sea: and the third part of the sea became blood;

9. And the third part of the creatures which were in the sea, and had life, died; and the third part of the ships were destroyed.

10. And the third angel sounded, and there fell a great star from heaven, burning as it were a lamp, and it fell upon the third part of the rivers, and upon the fountains of waters;

11. And the name of the star is called Wormwood: and the third part of the waters became wormwood; and many men died of the waters, because they were made bitter.

12. And the fourth angel sounded, and the third part of the sun was smitten, and the third part of the moon, and the third part of the stars; so as the third part of them was darkened, and the day shone not for a third part of it, and the night likewise.

13. And I beheld, and heard an angel flying through the midst of heaven, saying with a loud voice, Woe, woe, woe, to the inhabiters of the earth by reason of the other voices of the trumpet of the three angels, which are yet to sound!

Revelation 9:1,3,13-14

1. And the fifth angel sounded, and I saw a star fall from heaven unto the earth: and to him was given the key of the bottomless pit.

3. And there came...locusts upon the earth...

13. And the sixth angel sounded, and I heard a voice from the four horns of the golden altar which is before God,

14. Saying to the sixth angel which had the trumpet, Loose the four angels which are bound in the great river Euphrates...

CHAPTER 11

The Blowing of the First Six Trumpets

Until John receives the vision of the blowing of the trumpets, he heard many loud noises in Heaven. From God's throne came peals of thunder. The four living creatures called out, "Holy, holy, holy." The 24 elders sang. An innumerable host of angels worshipped God.

When the Lamb opens the seventh seal, there is a great dramatic silence.

The intensity of the scene is heightened by this complete absence of sound.

It might be that John hears Heaven quieted so the cries of God's persecuted servants can be heard. Some have thought that Heaven is silent so the prayers of God's persecuted children on earth can be heard in heaven.

But the majority of commentators take this silence to be the awesome silence before the storm of God's wrath breaks on the wicked. We can find the symbolism in the Old Testament, "But the LORD is in his holy temple: let all the earth keep silence before him" (Habakkuk 2:20). So awful is God's retribution that the inhabitants of Heaven stand spellbound for half an hour in breathless, silent amazement.

John sees an angel offer incense with the prayers of the saints. These are the prayers of God's people for vindication. Then the angel takes coals from the altar and throws them to the earth (Revelation 8:5). This is symbolic of how God hears the prayers of His persecuted people and how He will judge the wicked.

The Significance of Trumpets

Trumpets are significant musical instruments in Scripture. In Jewish life, Shofar trumpets (usually made of a ram's horn) were used as signaling instruments. We read in Numbers 10:2 that silver trumpets were used to call the congregation of Israel. They also sounded the alarm in time of war and announced religious feasts.

The Bible associates trumpets with the Day of the Lord. They herald the day of God's wrath, "A day of the trumpet and alarm against the fenced cities, and against the high towers. And I will bring distress upon men, that they shall walk like blind men, because they have sinned against the LORD: and their blood shall be poured out as dust, and their flesh as the dung" (Zephaniah 1:16-17).

Ecological Judgments

The first six trumpet judgments can be divided into two parts. The first four trumpet judgments are ecological judgments. The fifth and sixth trumpet blasts are demonic plagues.

The book of Revelation reveals ever-increasing, spiraling judgments. Revelation is like a musical theme with variations. Each variation adds something new to the whole composition.

These trumpet judgments recapitulate and develop the themes we already met in the running of the four horsemen. Revelation 6:8 told us that power was given to them over the fourth part of the earth. Now, we see an increase to one-third.

Seven angels execute the judgments of the seven trumpets. In I Enoch 20:2-8, an apocryphal book, reference is made to seven angels who stand before God. Their names are Gabriel, Michael – two angels mentioned in the Bible – as well as Uriel, Raphael, Raguel, Saraqael, and Remiel. We do not know the identity of the seven trumpet angels; we only know that they stand in the presence of God. Gabriel told Zacharias, "I am Gabriel, that stand in the presence of God" (Luke 1:19).

The First Trumpet

The blowing of the first trumpet led to the ecological destruction of houses, trees, and grass (Revelation 8:7). John saw a mighty thunderstorm bursting forth over the land accompanied by the fall of heavy hail along with fire mingled with blood. Tremendous lightning storms accompany it, which start fires and destroy the vegetable world.

This calamity reminds us of the seventh plague God brought upon Egypt (Exodus 9:24-26). That fire and hail were "cast upon the earth" implies that it was controlled in Heaven. The destruction of crops and trees means widespread famine and death. God shows His forbearance in destroying only one-third of the earth. Clearly, this great judgment has not yet come upon the earth, although, in history, God has sent widespread destruction and famine.

This future judgment will come in the period *of the last hour*. It will be in the period that immediately precedes the time of the final judgment.

The Second Trumpet

When the second angel sounded, John saw something like a great mountain burning with fire that was cast into the sea (Revelation 8:8).

This is a calamity defying description. Does a huge meteorite smash into the sea? This is an awe-inspiring symbol of maritime calamity, especially as the mountain is ablaze! The mountain could cause tremendous tidal waves sweeping away coastal cities. One-third of all marine creatures perish. One-third of all ships are destroyed, along with their passengers and crews. Oilrig platforms could be toppled. There is an incalculable loss of life and property. One-third of the sea is turned to blood. This reminds us of the first plague in Egypt when the Nile was turned into blood.

The Third Trumpet

When the third trumpet sounds, a great star called Wormwood pollutes inland waters (Revelation 8:10-11). Industry and commerce are affected. Wormwood is a shrub whose leaves are used to make a liqueur so toxic that its manufacture is banned in many countries. Wormwood is a plant with a bitter taste. So, the star is called Wormwood because of its embittering and poisoning effect upon lakes and rivers.

This is the reverse of the miracle at Marah, where the Lord made bitter waters sweet. This reminds us of how God polluted the Egyptians' drinking water.

The Fourth Trumpet

The fourth angel blows his trumpet and the sun, moon, and stars begin to function abnormally; their light is hidden. Perhaps massive volcanoes send ash into the atmosphere, obscuring the light of the sun. The temperatures of the world will plunge drastically. Weather patterns will be disrupted; crops will fail.

God is angry with men who have misused the creation. It is fitting that God's good creation and the bounties of providence begin to be taken away from sinful men who were unthankful.

The dimming of the lights sets the stage for an ominous announcement:

> And I beheld, and heard an angel flying through the midst of heaven, saying with a loud voice, Woe, woe, woe, to the inhabiters of the earth by reason of the other voices of the trumpet of the three angels, which are yet to sound! (Revelation 8:13).

What John actually sees is an "eagle." The imagery is of a strong bird of prey rushing to consume its victim.

The threefold "woe" is an expression of coming destruction. The inhabitants of the earth are the Christ-rejecters of the world. The Bible distinguishes the inhabitants of the earth from believers who are sojourners. These inhabitants are the people who try to make the earth their permanent dwelling. The eagle warns the wicked to pay attention, for they will encounter greater woes.

The Demonic Plagues

The fifth trumpet judgment is different from the four preceding. Rather than announcing an ecological plague, the fifth trumpet blast produces a demonic plague.

Demonic locusts from the abyss torture the inhabitants of the earth. Revelation 9:3-13 reveals their true identity and work. When the abyss is opened, huge billows of smoke pour out, darken the sky, and release horse-like locusts on the earth. Locust plagues are one of the severest plagues of mankind. The billows of smoke represent *the foulness* of the demons and their influence upon man.

These locusts are not ordinary earthly insects. They do not eat the grass; in fact, they are commanded not to hurt the grass of the earth. They do not cause damage with their mouths, but instead sting men with their scorpion tails.

John describes the locusts as an army of mounted troops that have unusual characteristics. Their faces resemble human faces; this suggests something unnatural, hence demonic. They have long hair like women; perhaps this is symbolic of the powers of seduction. They also have a leader who is called "Abaddon," which means "destroyer."

These are demons that come from the abyss. They do not kill man, but inflict agony like scorpion stings. They may not hurt those who have the seal of God on their foreheads. Their time of activity is limited to five months – the normal life span of the locust.

These demons play on the passions of men. Herman Hoeksema sees them as "spirits of pessimism." After men get caught up in sin, what follows in the wake is despair. All attempts to find joy and fulfillment in life, apart from God, lead in the end to a gloomy pessimism.

The devils will tempt men to experience the fleeting pleasures of sin that leave a nasty taste. They claim to deliver happiness and fulfillment, but leave people dangling, dissatisfied and bitter, in despair. These demons torture men, perhaps even more psychologically than physically.

Why would devils attack sinful men who are in their camp and already part of Satan's kingdom? This is a difficult question. But remember how the demons treated demoniacs in Jesus' day. They would throw a little boy in the fire or in water to drown him. They caused the Gadarene demoniacs to cut themselves and run around naked and live in tombs. They tormented men who were under their influence and will do so even more in the last days. Such is their maliciousness.

The Sixth Trumpet

The sixth trumpet blast results in the demonic slaughter of one-third of the inhabitants of the earth: "By these three was the third part of men killed, by the fire, and by the smoke, and by the brimstone, which issued out of their mouths" (Revelation 9:18).

A second woe is spoken which is a harbinger of even greater judgment. A voice comes from the horns of the golden altar, speaking to the sixth angel, "Loose the four angels which are bound in the great river Euphrates" (Revelation 9:14). These are four fallen angels who have been ordained as instruments of destruction.

The river represents the dividing line between the pagan nations and the geography of ancient Israel. Here it must be the dividing line between pagans and the false church. These four fallen angels relish the idea of plunging mankind into war. The four demons are loosed and an army of 200 million descends (Revelation 9:16).

John sees horses and horsemen with "breastplates of fire" that were jacinth (orange) and brimstone (yellow) (Revelation 9:17). The horses have lion's heads, symbolizing cruelty and destruction. From their mouths proceed fire, smoke, and sulfur – something that argues for their demonic origin. Like mythical dragons, they spew forth fire. A combination of hot lava and burning sulfur results in painful agony and death for all those in the destructive path of these warriors.

While some argue for a literal human army, several factors point to their identity as demonic forces. First, the tails that are like snakes' point to demonic creatures. Second, the impossibility of moving 200 million literal soldiers in the Middle East points to demons who could be present in such numbers. Third, smoke and fire come out of the mouths of the horses with lion's heads.

The result of the attack of these monsters is a war unparalleled in the annals of human history. Demons inspire people to destroy fellow humans with the most horrible weaponry at their disposal.

John records that in spite of God's plagues on the wicked world, men will not change: "And the rest of the men which were not killed by these plagues yet repented not of the works of their hands, that they should not worship devils" (Revelation 9:20), There is no repentance. There will be unbridled, unrestrained, escalating wickedness. The world will not improve as postmillennialists claim, it will grow worse.

Revelation 16:1-9

1. And I heard a great voice out of the temple saying to the seven angels, Go your ways, and pour out the vials of the wrath of God upon the earth.

2. And the first went, and poured out his vial upon the earth; and there fell a noisome and grievous sore upon the men which had the mark of the beast, and upon them which worshipped his image.

3. And the second angel poured out his vial upon the sea; and it became as the blood of a dead man: and every living soul died in the sea.

4. And the third angel poured out his vial upon the rivers and fountains of waters; and they became blood.

5. And I heard the angel of the waters say, Thou art righteous, O Lord, which art, and was, and shalt be, because thou hast judged thus.

6. For they have shed the blood of saints and prophets, and thou hast given them blood to drink; for they are worthy.

7. And I heard another out of the altar say, Even so, Lord God Almighty, true and righteous are thy judgments.

8. And the fourth angel poured out his vial upon the sun; and power was given unto him to scorch men with fire.

9. And men were scorched with great heat, and blasphemed the name of God, which hath power over these plagues: and they repented not to give him glory.

CHAPTER 12

The First Bowl Judgments: An Environmentalist's Worst Nightmare

Famines, floods, diseases, and earthquakes are signs of the return of Jesus Christ; our daily papers are full of these acts of God foretold by Jesus. "For nation shall rise against nation, and kingdom against kingdom: and there shall be famines, and pestilences, and earthquakes, in diverse places. All these are the beginning of sorrows" (Matthew 24:7-8). God is ratcheting up His judgments and will soon pour out the bowls of His wrath. Revelation 16 is a hair-raising chapter.

The bowl judgments occur when the Antichrist has established his worldwide kingdom. This will be a holocaust for confessing Christians and an end of the public witness of the church. God is pictured as telling seven angels to pour out bowls of wrath upon the earth and finally upon the kingdom of Antichrist.

The first four bowl judgments all have to do with judgments poured out upon nature. God uses these judgments to punish men who depend upon nature for food and drink. The "vials" in the King James Version should be imagined as shallow bowls. God tells the angels to pour out these bowls of wrath upon the earth.

The First Bowl Judgment

John sees the first angel pour out his bowl of wrath upon the earth (Revelation 16:2). This bowl is poured out on the dry land, and thus, the land is polluted.

God will send the judgment of disease and sickness – grievous sores. The word for "sore" comes from the Greek word from which we get the word "ulcer." We do not know what means God will use to give these grievous sores, but you can imagine that it will be like eating vegetables or fruit grown near Chernobyl. The food supply of the whole world will be polluted, resulting in sickness or starving to death.

The Second Bowl Judgment

John sees the second angel pour out his bowl of wrath upon the oceans and seas of the world (Revelation 16:3). The result is that they are corrupted and polluted.

Today, marine biologists worry about el Niños, coral reefs, and the extinction of endangered fish. With the first trumpet, one-third of the sea was turned to blood. Then one-third of the marine life died and one-third of ships were destroyed.

Now with the second bowl judgment, we find that in the end times, God will turn the entire sea into blood. Do marine biologists understand that there is going to be a worldwide extinction, far sooner than they could imagine?

God now deprives mankind of his livelihood from the oceans and seas of the world. There is an end to sea commerce. The dead fish and whales will rot on the beaches of the world.

The Third Bowl Judgment

The third bowl judgment is poured out upon the remaining sources of fresh water (Revelation 16:4). We do not know whether the rivers will be turned to literal blood, but the imagery is of the Exodus when God turned the Nile into blood.

We can scarcely conceive of the suffering of mankind as both the food and water supply are corrupted and become poisonous.

The Fourth Bowl Judgment

Then the fourth angel pours out his bowl of wrath on the sun. "And men were scorched with great heat, and blasphemed the name of God, which hath power over these plagues: and they repented not to give him glory" (Revelation 16:8-9).

In a world where mankind lacks fresh water, God compounds mankind's suffering by causing the sun to burn with a scorching heat. This sun-induced heatwave will be the like what man has never experienced. Man almost tastes the torments of hell.

Today, a great deal is said about the dangers of global warming. Scientists debate whether it is happening. They discuss whether there is a normal pattern of cooling down and warming up on planet earth or whether the use of fossil fuels is contributing to global warming.

In the 1970s, there were climate scientists who claimed that the world was about to enter another ice age. Now alarmists call for international treaties, like the Kyoto Treaty of Global Warming. Little do these alarmists realize that God promises to bring about a global warming such as no unbelieving scientist today can conceive.

The sun is the source of light and life on earth. In the end times, God causes it to become a destructive power. Men will be scorched with great heat. Can you imagine the results of this? The polar ice cap will melt. The oceans of the world will rise to inundate the great cities of the world with the blood of the oceans and the carcasses of tens of millions of marine life!

Today, environmentalism is sometimes elevated to the status of a religion. There is the Green Party with their utopia of a green earth. Unbelieving environmentalists view redemption in terms of saving the planet.

However, these catastrophic judgments are an environmentalist's worst nightmare. Their plans and hopes will all be dashed. God will judge mankind for how they have misused His creation. He will deal with the Chinese government for how they pollute the air and rivers in their great economic dash forward.

Just Revenge

God carries out a just revenge in these four bowl judgments. The judgments are so terrible and awe-inspiring and have such terrific and horrific consequences, that after the third plague, an angel of God feels the need to defend God's actions. "And I heard the angel of the waters say, Thou art righteous, O Lord, which art, and wast, and shalt be, because thou hast judged thus" (Revelation 16:5). John states, "And I heard another out of the altar say, Even so, Lord God Almighty, true and righteous are thy judgments" (Revelation 16:7).

The third plague is a prophetic judgment. The Antichrist and his followers have shed the blood of the saints. Now, these men will drink blood!

Think about this: who will be responsible for the destruction of all marine life? The answer: unbelieving scientists. The atheistic scientists who claim to be so supportive of protecting the environment are responsible for this future global warming. Their rebellion against the

Creator is why God will heat up the planet. Wicked scientists and politicians are to blame for the final, great extinctions. Sinners are responsible for what will happen. The world will deserve a destructive sun.

God's motive in the bowl judgments is to pour out the fullness of His wrath. This is evident in that the bowls are tipped over and their entire contents are emptied out. The number seven is a number of completeness or fullness.

When the seven seals are opened, the judgments affect one-fourth of the world. In the trumpet judgments, God affects one-third of the world. Now, no percentages are listed; God unleashes complete and full judgment on His enemies.

Men will acknowledge that these plagues come from the hand of Almighty God, for we read of them blaspheming the name of God. We would perhaps imagine that such severe judgments might soften the hearts of these sinners and cause them to repent in dust and ashes, but the opposite is true. "And men were scorched with great heat, and blasphemed the name of God, which hath power over these plagues, and they repented not to give him glory" (Revelation 16:9). We learn that absolutely nothing but the grace of God will humble a sinner.

Jesus says, "Behold, I come as a thief. Blessed is he that watcheth, and keepeth his garments, lest he walk naked, and they see his shame" (Revelation 16:15). Christ pronounces a beatitude. He speaks a blessing on the one who watches and keeps his garments.

To watch is to be prepared. In the parable of the prudent virgins, Jesus told the story of five wise virgins who were prepared for the arrival of the bridegroom (Matthew 25:1-13). The imagery in Revelation 16:15 is a bit different. It is not that of bridesmaids preparing for a wedding, but of a soldier alert and on duty.

Only a soldier who stays awake and keeps his clothes on is ready for combat. Those caught unprepared when the battle breaks out will walk about naked, and men will see their shame, the shame of a soldier derelict of his duty.

Between Christians and the thunderclouds of God's wrath stands the cross of Jesus Christ. Be sure that you are found in Christ so that you are not ashamed at His appearance.

12. And the sixth angel poured out his vial upon the great river Euphrates; and the water thereof was dried up that the way of the kings of the east might be prepared.

13. And I saw three unclean spirits like frogs come out of the mouth of the dragon, and out of the mouth of the beast, and out of the mouth of the false prophet.

14. For they are the spirits of devils, working miracles, which go forth unto the kings of the earth and of the whole world, to gather them to the battle of that great day of God Almighty.

15. Behold, I come as a thief. Blessed is he that watcheth, and keepeth his garments, lest he walk naked, and they see his shame.

16. And he gathered them together into a place called in the Hebrew tongue Armageddon.

CHAPTER 13

Har-Mageddon: The Last Battle

When we hear the name "Armageddon," what images does it conjure up? Do we think of an end time nuclear holocaust? Do we imagine children playing outside and then a nuclear blast causes their disintegration? What do we know about the battle of Armageddon? Who will fight? When and where will this fight occur?

The Location

"Armageddon" is a name that has passed into the popular imagination. It stirs up connotations of a last climactic world war. The word actually means "Mountain of Megiddo."

In the Bible, the name is pronounced "Har-Mageddon." "Megiddo" means "place of God." It was a city in Issachar or Manasseh, west of the Jordan River in the Plain of Jezreel. This location is mentioned a few times in the Bible. Jehu kills Ahaziah, the King of Judah, at Megiddo (II Kings 9:27). Pharoah-Necho killed King Josiah at Megiddo (II Chronicles 35:22).

There is a clear Old Testament allusion behind this reference to Armageddon in the book of Revelation. The symbol is rooted in the story found in Judges 4 and 5. Israel is in misery. King Jabin, the Canaanite, is the oppressor. His spoilers plunder the crops of Israel, sending the Israelites into hiding (Judges 5:6). King Jabin and his General Sisera are strong; they have 900 chariots of iron. Israel lacks basic weapons.

Deborah, the prophetess, brought God's word to Barak the judge. A battle was fought at Megiddo and Israel's enemy was routed. Jehovah Himself defeated them. "From heaven fought the stars; from their courses they fought against Sisera" (Judges 5:20). For this reason, Har-Megeddon is the symbol of every battle in which, when the need is the greatest and believers are oppressed; God suddenly comes to deliver them.

Something that has baffled commentators is the fact that apparently there is no mountain near Megiddo. There is only a valley. Perhaps it is symbolic of how armies usually wanted to fight from high ground.

It is not clear whether the last battle will literally be fought at Megiddo. Perhaps the location is symbolic of a world war fought on many fronts.

The Timing

The timing of the last battle will be the end of this dispensation. Repeatedly, the visions in Revelation lead us to the end of time. Again in this vision of the sixth vial, we are led to the very end of human history on the old planet earth. This battle occurs after the pouring out of the first five bowl judgments.

The Participants

Who will fight in the battle of Armageddon? It is not that the Antichrist fights against the true church of Jesus Christ. It is very strange, but many interpret Har-Mageddon to be a battle only between the Antichrist's kingdom and Christians. Perhaps this is because the day of the last battle is called "the battle of that great day of God Almighty" (Revelation 16:14).

It is true that at the end of the battle Jesus Christ, with His angelic army, takes on the assembled human warriors. But there are many problems with the idea that the last battle will be between the Antichrist and the true church. First, during the reign of Antichrist, the church has already been wiped out as a public institution. The Christians who were not martyred have fled to the hills. No large group of Christians remains on earth for Antichrist to attack.

Second, even if there were Christians on earth, they would not fight a literal, physical battle against Antichrist's forces. Christians do not fight with the sword for the kingdom, contrary to the history of the crusades. It would be foolish to think that Antichrist would gather his soldiers to fight against an invisible Christ. The two sides in this battle face human opponents.

The last battle begins as a war between formerly pagan countries and anti-Christendom. In the symbolism of the Euphrates River drying up and the kings of the east invading, we find the answer to the question: Who are the participants?

The Euphrates River is a symbol of the boundary between Old Testament Israel and her enemies. It is interesting that in Isaiah 8:7-8, we find symbolism of the Euphrates overflowing into Canaan as a picture of the Assyrian conquest of the ten tribes. Around the Euphrates River, the conquering armies of Assyria, Babylon, and Medo-Persian began their conquests. All of these nations were pagan.

When the Ephrates River is dried up, the road is prepared so that these pagan countries can attack Canaan. Now, we need to be careful at this point. One reason why people think that Har-Mageddon is a battle between Antichrist and Christians is because they get the symbolism wrong. They think that Gog and Magog are a picture of the Antichrist's kingdom attacking the church.

But the public witness of Christianity has ended. Instead, the Antichrist set up his world-religion as an institution. Jerusalem is the spiritual capital of his kingdom. We read: "And their dead bodies shall lie in the street of the great city, which spiritually is called Sodom and Egypt, where also our Lord was crucified" (Revelation 11:8). So Jerusalem is now a picture of the headquarters of the Antichrist's kingdom.

It is the Antichrist's kingdom that the kings of the east, Gog and Magog, now attack. We find a reference to Gog and Magog in Ezekiel 38:14-23. God gives Ezekiel a vision of fire and brimstone and the satisfying of His wrath. Here, we meet with this same Gog and Magog in Revelation, "And shall go out to deceive the nations which are in the four quarters of the earth, Gog and Magog, to gather them together to battle: the number of whom is as the sand of the sea" (Revelation 20:8).

The kings of the east and the kings of the earth who are mentioned in Revelation 16:12 and 14 are Gog and Magog. The Euphrates River is the symbolic boundary between anti- Christendom and paganism.

So, we have a picture of the final world war. The pagan nations (that would probably include India, China, the Islamic nations, and others) attack Antichrist. These are countries where Christianity never had a strong effect on the culture. These are nations that, for most of their history, plainly rejected Jesus of Nazareth. At first, the pagan nations will buy into the Antichrist's kingdom, but after a time they will rebel against it. Perhaps they rebel when the earth suffers under the judgments that God pours out upon the throne of the beast and on the creation.

In this last battle, we can only imagine the technology used. It is not as if the Euphrates River needs literally to dry up, but the picture is of God sovereignly removing any hindrances standing in the way of Gog and Magog being able to fight Antichrist. Fallen men will be at each other's throats. God, in His wrath against wicked, unrepentant mankind, will punish them with war. In this final, global battle there will be terrible destruction.

The Last Battle is a Divine Judgment, as is evident from the fact that it results from the pouring out of the fifth bowl.

Three Demonic Frogs

John sees demonic frogs who incite the battle of Armageddon:

> And I saw three unclean spirits like frogs come out of the mouth of the dragon, and out of the mouth of the beast, and out of the mouth of the false prophet. For they are the spirits of Devils, working miracles, which go forth unto the kings of the earth and of the whole world, to gather them to the battle of that great day of God Almighty (Revelation 16:13-14).

These frogs, jumping out of the mouth of the infernal trinity of the dragon, beast, and false prophet, picture the deceptive and deceiving speech of the false prophet.

As unclean spirits - demons - they spread out across the world, croaking the lies of the Devil. They are compared to frogs to indicate their abominable, loathsome, and repulsive character. Frogs were unclean: "Whatsoever hath no fins nor scales in the waters, that shall be an abomination unto you" (Leviticus 11:12).

These frogs are sent to do anti-missionary work. They "go forth unto the kings of the earth, and of the whole world, to gather them to the battle of that great day of God Almighty" (Revelation 16:14). The assumption is that there will be certain areas where anti-Christianity will catch on immediately, but other nations, especially those that are mostly pagan need to be the objects of anti-missionary work. These include the kings of the east mentioned in verse 12. So the frog-like demons are sent to the nations that live outside of the sphere of nominal Christianity. They are Gog and Magog.

In these nations, the demons proclaim their antichristian principles. They spread and sow the seed of conscious opposition against God and His Christ. They preach their infernal doctrines so that mankind might be united in his worship of the dragon.

However, God, who pours out the seven bowls, interrupts the Devil's plans. While the demons are trying to deceive the nations, the vials of God's wrath are poured out. God uses these frogs, which were meant to convert the pagans to Antichrist, as the means by which the nations become dissatisfied with Antichrist and turn on him.

We should not think of these bowls as being strictly successive. It seems that they occur together – at the end of time. They are related to each other and are gradually poured out. The first four bowls clearly belong together, being plagues in nature and wreaking havoc on the kingdom of Antichrist. Since people are no longer wealthy and healthy, they begin to have second thoughts about Antichrist.

The fifth bowl is poured out upon the throne of the Antichrist. His throne stands for the seat of his authority and power. It is a symbol of his universal rule. Antichrist was enthroned by the popular will of the nations. People trusted him as a god and worshiped his image. Man had created paradise on earth.

But now God causes the dominion of the Antichrist to be darkened. The result of the bowl being poured is that "his kingdom was full of darkness; and they gnawed their tongues for pain" (Revelation 16:10). This is not just darkness in nature, for that could not be harmonized with the scorching heat of the sun from the fourth vial. What it symbolizes is that the authority of Antichrist is questioned, and he loses power.

Weakness Perceived in the Antichrist

The nations used to say, "Who can make war with the beast?" But now they are not so sure of his unconquerable power. These nominally pagan nations were never really into his philosophy and religion. They followed him for the material blessings, but now, because of God's plagues, they have lost this motivation for following Antichrist.

The darkening of the throne of the beast will result in an uprising against Antichrist. The nations at the four corners of the earth will wake up and realize their hearts were never totally sold on Antichrist's doctrines. They will then want to destroy the beast and do away with his authority.

This is the battle to end all battles. As the seventh vial is poured out, God begins to refine the earth. A great voice is heard from the throne of God saying: "It is done." Jesus, on the cross, shouted out: "It is finished." In *principle* it was finished, but now in *reality*, "It is finished."

In the middle of this world war, Jesus Christ will return. The significance of this battle is that it is the battle to end all battles. It is the victory of Jesus Christ.

At Har-Mageddon, Jesus Christ has a final mighty clash with the Antichrist and the wicked world. As the nations are at each other throats, Christ will suddenly appear and take them both to task. He will fight on behalf of His beleaguered saints. Christ will appear riding on a white horse and on His thighs the names written: "King of Kings and Lord of Lords."

The very name "Armageddon" reminds us of God giving the Israelites, under Deborah and Barak, victory over King Jabin. We think of Jael, first such a good hostess, then nailing a spike through Sisera's head. In the last battle, the Seed of the woman will crush the head of the seed of the serpent.

The Living God fights against the wicked. A great earthquake destroys the city of this world. The islands disappear and the mountains melt at the presence of God, the Lord of all the earth. One hundred pound hailstones fall out of Heaven (Revelation 16:21). And all of this was very remarkably predicted in Ezekiel 38:18-23.

At the end, Christ will recreate the world and set up an everlasting kingdom of peace!

The White Horse Rider: the Judge of Terrorists

After September 11, 90 percent of the American people supported military action to punish the terrorist organization that perpetrated this crime, as well as any countries that might have given aided, supported, and harbored them. On the other hand, I heard a child saying that she did not want the United States to punish the terrorists because that would make them mad – and they might commit more terrorist attacks.

Is there Biblical support for declaring war on the terrorists and their host nations? In response to questions like this, Christians have developed the Just War Theory. Christ Jesus, today, uses nations to judge terrorists, but in the end, the Lord Christ will take justice into His own hands.

Throughout Christian history, the most anticipated future event has been the personal return of Jesus Christ. At the end of the Bible, John sees a glorious Rider (Revelation 19). From His appearance, it is evident that the horseman is a Great Conqueror. He rides a white horse and is crowned with a diadem – a crown of absolute sovereignty. A sharp sword protrudes from His mouth. His eyes blaze like fire.

The Donkey King Versus the White-Horse-Rider

What is remarkable is the contrast between this glorious White-Horse-Rider and His former appearance. He once rode a little donkey into Jerusalem. He walked the dusty roads of Palestine. He felt the hot sun on His neck. He was hungry. He was abused. Finally, He was crucified like a common criminal.

That the White-Horse-Rider is a victorious general is evident from the whole scene. Victorious generals often rode white steeds to celebrate a triumph since white is a picture of victory. This horseman is the leader of a great, victorious army. Enoch prophesied about Him: "I saw the Lord coming with tens of thousands of his saints" (Jude 14).

The blazing eyes of the Rider speak of full discernment and penetrating knowledge. His eyes penetrate into the heart of men. He is fair in judgment. Nothing can be hidden from His gaze.

In the next chapter, we meet the same person: "And I saw a great white throne, and him that sat on it, from whose face the earth and the heaven fled away; and there was found no place for them" (Revelation 20:11). The white horse Rider is the Judge of terrorists. He will preside over the great white throne judgment. He terrorizes the wicked.

His Exalted Names

That the White-Horse-Rider is Jesus of Nazareth is evident from the names given to Him. He has a name written that no man knew, but Himself (Revelation 19:11). This shows the mysterious depths of the Rider. We can understand a few things about who the White-Horse-Rider is, but we are too limited to penetrate into the depths of this One who is God and who is man. There is a name that is too special for us to hear or too profound for us to understand.

The Rider is identified as "The Word of God." Is it because John saw this that he began his gospel account, "In the beginning was the Word?" (John 1:1). The Rider is the second person of the holy Trinity. He is the Word who always was with God and who is God. He is the One by whom all things were created.

The Rider is "Faithful and True." He is "Faithful." He returns as He promised. He can be relied upon. He is "True." The Antichrist is a fraud. The opposite of being true or ideal is being spurious, false, or imperfect. He is the Perfect Ruler. Christ is who He claims to be: God's Son – the Messiah.

The White-Horse-Rider has a name written on His clothing and on His thigh (the clothing on His thigh) "KING of KINGS, and LORD of LORDS." This is truly "the name high over all." Christ has absolute supremacy! He is owed allegiance by Osama bin Laden, Putin, and President Bush.

The LORD of LORDS is also a Lover, the Bridegroom of the church. Christ returns to marry His bride. Samuel Rutherford wrote:

> The Bride eyes not her garments,
> But her dear Bridegroom's face.
> And I will not gaze at glory,
> But on my King of Grace.
> Not at the crown he giveth,
> But on his pierced hands,
> The Lamb is all the glory
> Of Emmanuel's' land.

In righteousness, Jesus Christ returns to judge and make war. This is the climax of all history. Here is a combination of war and judgment. Jesus carries out justice through war – at the climax of the Battle of Armageddon.

The Wrath of the Lamb

In flaming fire, Christ takes vengeance on His enemies. The thought of Christ's return should comfort you:

> And to you who are troubled rest with us, when the Lord Jesus shall be revealed from heaven with his mighty angels, In flaming fire taking vengeance on them that know not God, and that obey not the gospel of our Lord Jesus Christ: Who shall be punished with everlasting destruction from the presence of the Lord, and from the glory of his power (II Thessalonians 1: 7-9).

Jesus will make war with reprobate men, the Antichrist, and the devils. The Word wars with words. He does not use a physical weapon. The simple word spoken is sufficient. Martin Luther sang that "one little word shall fell" the Devil. Paul says that Jesus will "consume with the spirit of his mouth."

Jesus carries out righteous judgment. The "rod of iron" is a symbol of tough justice, of unbending, unwavering righteousness. Paul said that He would take vengeance on them that "obey not the gospel of our Lord Jesus Christ."

There is too much "easy-believism" around us. Christians in America call upon people to believe in Christ, but they do not call upon people to obey what Jesus commanded! Jesus said if you love Him, then keep His commandments.

Christ will return as a Man of War. When Moses saw Pharaoh and his armies drowned in the Red Sea, he sang, "The LORD is a man of war" (Exodus 15:3). Jesus rides forth in majesty, power, and great glory "conquering and to conquer." Jesus has a controversy with sinful men and devils.

The Rider has vesture dipped in blood. This pictures how Jesus will shed the blood of the wicked, for "he treadeth the winepress of the fierceness and wrath of Almighty God" (Revelation 19:15).

A remarkable dialogue is found in the 63rd chapter of Isaiah between the prophet and the Warrior-Messiah. As Isaiah is shown the coming of Christ, he stands in Jerusalem looking to the south toward Edom. He sees a great warrior coming with garments stained red (Isaiah 63:1-4).

The Son of God is filled with "fierce wrath." Literally, John speaks of His rage, His settled anger. The Greek word translated "rage" means "exploding, volatile wrath, anger in action." The other word "orge" refers to the settled anger of God against sin that proceeds from His unalterable holiness.

Evil and evil men are still in the world, but the Bible is clear that the wages of sin is death. After September 11, 2001, it was interesting how commentators talked about the reality of evil. It seems that the sinful world wants to get the word "sin" out of the public sphere and out of the human vocabulary. But events like September 11 remind us of the terrible reality of sin. Attempts at mass murder betray the evil found in fallen human nature.

Christ will return to punish evildoers. The terrorists, who flew the passenger jets into the World Trade Center, fooled themselves into thinking that by their suicide attack, they would gain Paradise and numerous virgins. Jesus has already cured them of that idea. He reveals His anger to the wicked at the moment of their death, casting them into Hell. The sinner will pay unless he is an elect sinner whose sins were atoned for by the Lamb.

Having vanquished the enemies of His bride, Christ rescues her in order to marry her. Jesus' return ushers in two dinners. The first is a rather revolting meal – vultures gorge upon the flesh of the wicked. John sees Jesus calling upon the eagles and vultures to gather for a dinner of human corpses. This imagery presents the final indignity for wicked men. This is expressive of complete defeat, disgrace, and shameful public subjection of the enemies of God.

The saints celebrate God's justice in judging the great whore. Be assured and aware that there is an appointed day when God will judge all men by the Man Christ Jesus. A place of eternal torment waits, where every rebel and every unbeliever will suffer the wrath of God.

The second dinner is the long-awaited marriage supper of the Lamb. Note how the wedding supper is called that of the Lamb, emphasizing Christ's atoning death as the basis for the marriage. By His cross, Jesus paid the dowry for His bride.

John is overwhelmed by the power of the spontaneous worship of the heavenly hosts. Angels and saints are filled with gladness. All opposition has been quenched forever. The saints give expression to joy by crying, "Hallelujah!" Their hearts are filled with ecstasy to the breaking point. John also hears a solo voice, probably that of a cherubim or a mighty angel exclaiming, "Praise our God, all ye his servants, and ye that fear him, both small and great" (Revelation 19:5). The innumerable lips of Heaven, sounding like the voice of many waterfalls, cry out, "Alleluia: for the Lord God omnipotent reigneth. Let us be glad and rejoice and give honor to Him: for the marriage of the Lamb is come, and His wife hath made herself ready" (Revelation 19:6-7). All of the hallelujahs of Heaven seem to be let loose.

Imagine all the mighty waterfalls and ocean waves, all the choirs, and all the thunders of the world sounding forth at the same time. You still have only a fraction of what the praise of Heaven will sound like on the Last Day!

The saints praise God for vindicating His name and His glory and His truth.

When John has seen the visions of God's judgment of Babylon and hears the praise of Heaven and hears about the marriage supper of the Lamb, he is stunned. He falls down and starts to worship the angel who showed him this revelation.

The angel stops him and tells him to worship God. God is the One who has destroyed the city of this world. Our worship should be a public savoring of the greatness of the God who will deliver us from the sinful world. Our worship should be a flagrant enjoyment of the righteousness of God.

Made in the USA
Monee, IL
10 December 2024

71317575R00085